Rethinking Literary Biography

Rethinking Literary Biography

A Postmodern Approach to Tennessee Williams

Nicholas Pagan

Rutherford • Madison • Teaneck
Fairleigh Dickinson University Press
London and Toronto: Associated University Presses

Associated University Presses
440 Forsgate Drive
Cranbury, NJ 08512

Associated University Presses
25 Sicilian Avenue
London WC1A 2QH, England

Associated University Presses
P.O. Box 338, Port Credit
Mississauga, Ontario
Canada L5G 4L8

The paper used in this publication meets the requirements
of the American National Standard for Permanence of Paper
for Printed Library Materials Z39.48-1984.

Library of Congress Cataloging-in-Publication Data

Pagan, Nicholas, 1953–
    Rethinking literary biography : a postmodern approach to Tennessee
Williams / Nicholas Pagan.
        p.   cm.
    Includes bibliographical references and index.
    ISBN 0-8386-3516-4
    1. Williams, Tennessee, 1911–1983—Criticism and interpretation.
    2. Postmodernism (Literature)—United States.   3. Autobiography in
literature.   4. Intertextuality.   I. Title.
PS3545.I5365Z798   1993
812'.54—dc20   92-55117
                                                                                      CIP

To Kathleen

The subject is absolutely indispensable. I don't destroy the subject; I situate it.

—Jacques Derrida

After he dressed, I helped him pack. He asked me if I wanted the college textbooks with his plays inside. He very proudly showed me the books, opening them to their indexes, reading out the names of his plays. "They study me in universities all over America," he told me, "they do, baby. I don't think you knew that."

I told him I had studied his plays at Columbia.

"There, too?" he smiled, pleased. "You see I am not finished yet. The critics can attack me but a whole new generation . . .?" He shrugged.

—Dotson Rader

Contents

Preface

One day while packing, Tennessee Williams and his friend, Dotson Rader, found themselves looking through college textbooks. Finding the names of his plays listed in the indexes, Williams declared gleefully, "They study me in universities all over America." Devastated so many times by merciless critical reviews, he wondered about "a whole new generation."[1] As a member of this "new generation," I decided that I would not try to judge Tennessee Williams's plays (or other works), and I would certainly not attack Tennessee Williams. Instead, I would speculate about the relationship between the "me," the Tennessee Williams studied throughout America, and the "me," the texts, whether literary or nonliterary, to which he has affixed his name.

Soon, though, I became interested, not so much in Tennessee Williams or his work, or, indeed, the relationship between the two "me"s, but in the relationship between an author (any author) and his or her texts. I observed that many of the scholars working in the field of literary biography had turned to language as the primary element in literary biography, and I felt that the linguistic turn was also characteristic of a good deal of contemporary critical theory. Nevertheless, although we are now presented with a superabundance of theory and criticism of literature, theater, film, architecture, and so on, there is a marked paucity of critical theory of biography, and the quantity of biographical criticism is minuscule compared with the quantity of literary criticism.

Here, then, I try to imagine what form literary biography might take if it were responsive to the developments in critical theory found especially in the work of Roland Barthes and Jacques Derrida. These thinkers have questioned the notion of straightforward filiation. Barthes, for example, specifies that the work and the life are "the substance of a *connection,* and not a *filiation.*"[2] Instead of examining the author or the author's psyche, then, as source/origin/father of the author's texts, these thinkers claim that the author's life is itself a

text. Traditional biographers and traditional biographical theorists frequently talk about reanimating dead bones, breathing fresh life into
the author, or of capturing or recapturing that life. These are the
clichés of traditional biography. Postmodern thinkers, like Barthes,
however, replace the flesh and blood author with "a paper-author,"[3]
and argue that the flesh and blood author is inaccessible; or, at least,
is knowable only as a function of discourse, not as a pre-linguistic
entity.

I am proposing a revisioning of literary biography in line with some
of this Continental thought. From Barthes, then, I adapt the notion
that the relationship between authors and their texts is not one of
filiation but of connection, and this leads me to explore the concept
of intertextuality. From Derrida, I adapt the idea that texts are engendered on the border between author and text, and I suggest that
the author (the "paper-author") may enter the intertextual network
through the play of a proper name. From Derrida, I also borrow the
concept of signature, which manifests itself through different modalities. The kind of literary biography that I have in mind, not only
provides a new way for literary biography to consider the relation
between author and text, but also offers the would-be literary biographer a new way of creating his or her own texts.

As well as attempting to fill the gap in literary biography caused
by its relative neglect by critical theory, I am attempting to offer a
study of the relationship between one particular author, Tennessee
Williams, and his texts. William Gass once remarked that "Faulkner's
life was nothing until it found its way into Faulkner's language."[4] We
may be tempted to say the same thing about Tennessee Williams.
After all, who would care about Tennessee Williams's life if he were
not the author of *The Glass Menagerie, A Streetcar Named Desire*,
and so on. In the kind of postmodern literary biography that I am
envisaging, however, it is not a question of an author's life finding its
way into his or her language because the author's life is always already
language.

Whereas some writers have deliberately shunned the public eye
(a most notable example is Samuel Beckett), others, like Tennessee
Williams, have courted the public eye with astonishing persistence.
Perhaps one consequence of this is the existence, as we shall see, of
a plethora of autobiographical and biographical material. As far as
Williams's own statements are concerned, though, they should, of
course, not be taken as absolute truths. Any author may be regarded

as inventing his or her own life, and as Norman K. Denzin observes, "if an author can make up facts about his or her life, who is to know what is true and what is false?"[5] Nevertheless, I frequently refer to statements made by Williams—especially statements occurring in interviews. This is partly why I adopt the notion of text rather than work. "The text must not be confused with the work," says Barthes, "A work is a finished object, something computable, which can occupy a physical space. . . . The work is held in the hand, the text in language."[6] The term *text,* then, is more all-encompassing than work. It enables me to move with ease from Williams's overtly literary material—plays, fiction, poems—to his memoirs, essays, letters and interviews, any situation in fact where Williams employs language.

I should emphasize that my concern is not with the interpretation of individual texts (i.e., the concern of traditional literary criticism), although some interpretation may occur along the way. My concern, rather, as I have said, is the connection between texts and author. Williams's texts and his life (constituted by and in language) playfully traverse a scene of writing that becomes the enigmatic site of my personal reading.

Notice that I say, "playfully." Although the usefulness of play has been questioned by traditional philosophy and generally regarded as insufficiently serious by aficionados of modernism, the postmodern approach to literary biography that I am advocating revels in play. Although authors are dead, as paper-authors, they are not static, but are always involved in an active, on-going, and playful relation with their texts. They are involved in a game, however, which only succeeds to the extent that we as readers are prepared to enter it.

Acknowledgments

I began working on this book at the University of Florida. I would like to thank the many friends and colleagues there who, sometimes knowingly, sometimes unknowingly, have greatly contributed to the development of this project. In particular, I must thank Jesús Mejía, who led me to Williams in the first place and whose friendship has been invaluable. I would also like to thank Megan Wall, William Jernigan, and Harvey Molloy. John Seelye and Anne Goodwyn Jones were helpful in responding to my tentative initial efforts. My dissertation director, Sidney Homan, also responded in detail to earlier drafts and was unflinchingly enthsiastic about the project. I owe a special debt to John P. Leavey Jr., who seemed always available to talk theory, and who continued to respond to work in progress after I moved from the University of Florida to Auburn University.

Permission has been granted by New Directions Publishing Corporation for use of quotations from the following works by Tennessee Williams:

Battle of Angels. Copyright 1940, 1945 by Tennessee Williams.
Cat on a Hot Tin Roof. Copyright 1954, 1955 by Tennessee Williams.
Camino Real. As *Ten Blocks on the Camino Real* (a one-act play) copyright 1948 by Tennessee Williams. As *Camino Real,* revised and published version, copyright 1953 by Tennessee Willaims.
The Glass Menagerie. Copyright 1945 by Tennessee Williams and Edwina D. Williams.
Night of the Iguana. Copyright 1961 by Two Rivers Enterprises, Inc.
Orpheus Descending. Copyright 1955, 1958 by Tennessee Williams.
A Streetcar Named Desire. Copyright 1947 by Tennessee Williams.
Summer and Smoke. Copyright 1948 by Tennessee Williams.

Rethinking Literary Biography

1

Literary Biography's Quest for the Biographical Subject

Literary biography is still new enough as an art to be hospitable to experimentation, as a scholarly discipline it is malleable enough to be responsive to new intellectual tendencies as they appear.
—Richard D. Altick

Anyone turning biographer has committed himself to lies, to concealment, to hypocrisy, to flattery, and even to hiding his own lack of understanding: for biographical truth is not to be had, and even if it were, it couldn't be useful.
—Sigmund Freud

Literary biography has never been easy to define. Widely acknowledged as one of the most important contributors both to the practice and discussion of biography, Leon Edel, seems to offer a straightforward definition when he describes "literary biography" as "the writing of the lives of men and women who were themselves writers."[1] There is, however, an obvious ambiguity in this definition. If we place the emphasis on the "who were themselves writers" part of the definition, then it implies that any work whose subject is the life of a literary man or woman is automatically "literary biography;" but if we place the emphasis on the first part of the definition, "the writing of the lives," then the term *literary biography* is only appropriate when the subject-matter manifests itself through a certain style of writing that is itself somehow deemed "literary."

Another important contributor to the discussion of biography, Richard Altick, emphasizes this second aspect of the definition when he suggests that "literary biographies are more successful than others [i.e., other kinds of biography] because they are couched in the language of the art in which they deal."[2] Thus, literary biographies are superior to the biographies of, for example, painters or sculptors because biographers (at least, in terms of our familiar conception of them) cannot paint or sculpt their subjects; but if their subjects are literary, biographer and subject are automatically working with a common entity: language. This does not mean that biographers and their subjects need to employ the same genre—if the literary biographer is writing about a novelist, the biography has to resemble that of a novel; if a dramatist, the biography has to resemble that of a play et cetera. The point seems to be a more general one—that literary language is so wonderful that it will automatically find its way into the literary biography and elevate it above the biographies whose subjects are not men or women of letters.

During the twentieth century some people concerned about such matters have regarded literary biography as an art while others have seen it as a science. Either one of these extremes may account for the tendency to elevate the status of literary biography.

In the early years, thinkers like Sidney Lee insisted on discussing biography in terms of craft. He saw biography as "a compilation, an industriously elaborated composition, a mosaic," and emphasized the biographer's need to rely on facts. A marked contrast to this view is provided by Edmund Gosse, who felt that biography was closer to art and described biography as "a branch of literature."[3] In the Twenties, Harold Nicholson tried to pull biography further away from craft or science by pointing to the danger of too much science seeping into biography. He maintained that "scientific interest in biography is hostile to literary interest and will in the long run destroy it."[4]

All three thinkers seemed to agree that the task of biography was to convey the individual personality of the subject, but the obvious problem faced in particular by Gosse and Nicholson was how to convey the enigmatic truth of individuality without relying on craft or science.[5] This point was taken up by Virginia Woolf, who in "The New Biography" explains biography's dilemma in these memorable terms,

> On the one hand there is truth; on the other there is personality. And if we think of truth as something of granite-like solidity and of personality as something of rainbow-like intangibility and reflect that the aim of biography is to weld these two into one seamless whole, we shall admit that the problem is a stiff one.[6]

Although Woolf certainly believes in these "granite-like" facts and regards biography as a craft and not an art, she acknowledges that "facts must be manipulated; some must be brightened; others shaded; yet, in the process, they must never lose their integrity."[7] She also sees the biographer being pulled away from truth in the direction of fiction:

> for it would seem that the life that is increasingly real to us is the fictitious life; it dwells in the personality rather than in the act. . . . Thus, the biographer's imagination is always being stimulated to use the novelist's art of arrangement, suggestion, dramatic effect to expound the private life. Yet if he carries the use of fiction too far, so that he disregards the truth, or can only introduce it with incongruity, he loses both worlds; he has neither the freedom of fiction nor the substance of fact.[8]

Woolf, then, contrasts the inner life, which is intangible, having a "rainbow-like" quality, with the life of action, which is seemingly concrete, "granite-like;" and she believes that both are important. Nevertheless, what James Joyce's famous biographer, Richard Ellman, would later declare to be his objective, "the inner life," "the obscure life" of his subject, Woolf argues has a dreamlike fictitious quality about it.[9] Thus, it is possible to see facts as leading not to more reality, but to fiction.

Our thinking on literary biography in the twentieth century has continued to vacillate between what Nicholson called "the strident streets of science" and "the open fields of fiction," between the poles of the scientific and the literary, between pretensions toward facticity on the one hand and acknowledgment of the inevitability of fiction on the other.

About fifty years after Woolf penned her thoughts on biography a fictional biographer in a work of fiction, Dubin in Malamud's *Dubin's Lives,* would declare that "there is no life that can be recaptured wholly; as it was. Which is to say that all biography is ultimately fiction."[10] Malamud's text questions the romantic idea or ideal of bringing the dead author back to life. Attempting to write a life of D. H. Lawrence, Dubin expresses the biographer's awful predicament in these terms:

> The dead poet was terribly real. He felt an imperious need to state his sorrow, understanding, pity—wanted with all his heart to preserve the man from extinction. Dubin, you can't relight lives but you can re-create them. In biographies the dead become alive, or seem to.[11]

Here the emphasis is on the process of writing, writing not as the listing of cold facts, but as transformative, creative, or more precisely, recreative. Notice the "or seem to," for obviously the dead are not really coming back to life; the biographer must rely on illusion, on fiction.

Paul Murray Kendall describes biography as "the craft-science-art of the impossible" and the biographer as "a man who fails before he begins."[12] "The fundamental emotion that powers biographical practice," writes Kendall, "is surely the desire to mark, to keep alive, the passage of a man by recapturing the life of that man. . . ."[13] We might question the notion of "recapturing," for surely we cannot assume that a life can ever be captured, even by the person living it, so how can it be recaptured?

There seems to be a ubiquitous belief, however, that "biography can deliver the essential person and that there is what Justin Kaplan calls "a core personality, the 'real Me,' which we will find if only we dig deep and long enough."[14] Toward the end of Malamud's book, Dubin finds himself attempting to explain his life as a biographer to a psychiatrist:

> "When you write biography you want to write about people who will make you strain to understand them." Dubin said it was like chasing a runner you would never catch up with. "But the game is, I suppose, to make the reader think that's exactly what you have done, and maybe in a blaze of illumination even have outdistanced him. It's an illusory farce that holds me by the tail."[15]

Despite the farcical nature of their project, literary biographers continue to be held by the tail, and, indeed, have not shied away from making grandiose claims for "literary biography." Writing in 1957, Edel maintains that with "literary biography" one can learn "every secret of a writer's soul, every quality of a writer's mind."[16] About twenty years later, however, we find Edel substituting for the soul, the notion of "personal myth."[17] One can approach the "personal myth," sometimes called "life myth," by reading "certain psychological signs that enable us to understand what people are really saying behind the faces they put on. . . ."[19] It is possible, according to Edel, to see behind the mask, to see "the figure under the carpet," in short, to discover "the essence of a life."[19] The successful accomplishment of this task, however, will only be possible if the biographer incorporates psychoanalytic psychology.[20]

Whether he talks in terms of soul, personal myth, or essences, Edel seems propelled by a belief in the biographer's ability to get at a preexisting referent. His claims are obviously emotional, romantic, and rely on a faith that has nourished the biographer, sustained his enthusiasm, and enabled him to exhibit an unflinching dedication to his task.

Part of the biographer's enthusiasm may be found in the frequently held belief in cross-fertilization between biography and criticism, the belief that literary biography can contribute to literary criticism and vice-versa. Writing in 1927, Alan C. Valentine suggested that

> The most successful biographies are those in which what a man wrote is brought in only incidentally to throw light upon his career and his character; the most successful pieces of literary criticism are found when the writer is looking first at a piece of literature and only through that at the man who created it.[21]

Notice that although in a sense Valentine attempts to separate the two activities: biography and criticism, he is reluctant to do so completely. What, we may ask, does "brought in only incidentally" mean? How can one separate what is essential from what is "brought in only incidentally"? Similarly, how can one respect a rigid temporal order, considering first the literature and then the man. In literary criticism there are numerous instances of critics disparaging the work because of a dislike of the man, at least the man the critics think they know. Perhaps the best known is T. S. Eliot and F. R. Leavis's attack on Milton's work. Their attack seems to be based on their obvious dislike of Milton, the man.

Altick rightly points out that "in the period from approximately 1915 to 1950 . . . some of the most influential critics maintained that a work of art is autonomous and complete in itself, and that any discussion of the author as a person is, for critical purposes, irrelevant and actually mischievous." Of course, the old New Critics used to focus on the literary text as an object, as a "well-wrought urn," severed from its author. In 1952, however, Leslie Fiedler urged readers to connect writer and work: "'Only connect!'" said Fiedler, "should be the motto of all critics and teachers—and the connective link between the poem on the page and most of its rewarding contexts is precisely—biography." Altick himself argues that "whenever the study of literary genetics succeeds in throwing even a tiny fresh beam upon a poem, we are by that much the richer."[22]

Frequently the writers themselves speak out against a biographical approach to their work. Edel has often referred to Auden's remarks about biography as being "always superfluous" and "usually in bad taste."[23] Petrie singles out Dickens, James, and Faulkner as examples of those "notorious for their attempts to protect their private lives by trying to separate them from the lives of their writings."[24] In the case of Faulkner, however, the great writer does not deny the connection altogether. Petrie quotes a letter form Faulkner to Joan Williams contained in Blotner's biography of Faulkner: "Now I realize for the first time what an amazing gift I had. . . . I wonder if you have ever had that thought about that work and the country man whom you know as Bill Faulkner—what little connection there seems to be between them."[25] Even if "little," Faulkner does not deny that there is a connection.

In 1981, we find Edel still advocating biography's ties to mythology. In "Biography and the Science of Man," he argues that "a life-myth is hidden within every poet's work," and he talks about the need to find "keys" to the "private mythology of the individual."[26] The obvious place to look for the myth is in the writer's work. In fact, at the beginning of the essay, Edel says, "I am not sure that the work and the life can be disassociated. As St. Beuve reminds us, *tel arbre, tel fruit.*"[27] Furthermore, 1982 sees the publication of *Henry James: The Middle Years: 1882–1895* in which Edel argues that "above all, Henry James issued an invitation to biographers to seek out the artist in 'the invulnerable granite' of his art." "I have accepted this invitation," says Edel, "because this is where the artist should be sought."[28] With his choice of the word "granite" Edel revisits Virginia Woolf's metaphor and reminds us of her exhortation concerning the importance of solid facts. The granite, the monumentality is to be found not in the world outside then, but in the work of art. Despite the earlier hesitancy, the ostensible lack of certainty, it is clear that Edel passionately believes in the connection between writer and work, and he has become, perhaps, the most well-known advocate of the biographical approach to literature. The following year he again quotes James to corroborate his view. James argued that "the artist is present in every page of every book." Edel maintains that to discover this presence the biographer doubles as critic. Edel strongly believes that the writer stamps his effigy on every coin that he mints and that "the man is the style." Countering the New Criticism's refusal to see that the poet is his poem, the novelist is his novel, Edel argues that there are "invisible threads . . . which bind [the work] to the fashioning mind."[29]

I contend that there are no set rules governing the writing of literary biography. Indeed, one of the virtues of literary biography is that it
allows for a healthy variety of styles. What brings literary biographies
together into a genre (sometimes called a subgenre) is their common
referent: a literary man or woman. How biographers construct this
literary man or woman will vary, but it is important to bear in mind
that they always construct this referent. Although the biographical
project is an impossible one, it should certainly not be abandoned. On
the contrary, it should be reexamined, rethought, and new ways of
thinking about and practicing biography should be brought to light.

*   *   *

The need to consider the connection between writer and work is not
only felt by biographers and biographical theorists but also, as we
have seen, by the literary artists themselves. Our subject, Tennessee
Williams, is an example of a writer who frequently talks outside his
writings of the writer/work relationship. Thus, although he claims
that he loves "revising and revising because it delays the moment
when there is this separation between you and your work,"[30] he also
seems to believe that this separation is not absolute because elsewhere
he says, "If the writing is honest it cannot be separated from the man
who wrote it."[31] Furthermore, in a review of Paul Bowles's *The Delicate Prey and Other Stories,* he asks, "what would lyricism be without
a personal accent?" (WL, 36). In *Memoirs,* he contends that "all true
work is personal, whether directly or obliquely, it must and does reflect
the emotional climates of its creator" (MS, 188). This view suggests
that Williams, like Edel, cannot separate the work from the author's
personality, the author's psychological makeup.

Speaking about his own experience, in an interview for *Newsweek*
in 1957, after admitting that writing is for him "a form of therapy,"
Williams talks about writing from his own tensions: "I can't handle
people in routine situations. I must find characters who correspond
to my own tensions."[32] In "Person to Person" (1955), he again stresses
his view that "so much of all creative work is so closely tied to the
personality of the one who does it," and he goes on to explain his
theory of "personal lyricism":

> I once saw a group of girls on a Mississippi side-walk, all dolled up in their
> mothers' and sisters' finery, old raggedy ball gowns and plumed hats. . . .
> But one child was not satisfied with the attention paid her enraptured

> performance by the others, they were too involved in their own perform-
> ances to suit her, so she stretched out her skinny arms and threw back her
> skinny neck and shrieked to the deaf heavens and her equally oblivious
> playmates, "Look at me, look at me, look at me!" (CT, vii; WL, 75–76)

Williams suggests that this may be "a parable of all artists." In other words, through their work artists draw attention to themselves; over and over again throughout their work, artists are saying, "Look at me, look at me, look at me!" This yoking of artist and work is very much in keeping with some of the theoretical speculations I have been discussing, and it also reflects approaches taken by many of Williams's biographers and critics of Williams's plays.

In *Tennessee Williams: The Man and His Work* (1961), Benjamin Nelson analyzes the works for "themes, techniques, and basic beliefs which endow them with their particular and highly individualistic character." He feels that he is able to discover the author's beliefs through the works. Although Signi Falk in *Tennessee Williams* (1961; revised 1978) in keeping with the New Critical dogma criticizes the fact that the plays are read as part of Tennessee Williams's personal history, she herself argues that writing for Williams is "a form of psychotherapy," and she seems unable to avoid reading the plays as part of the author's "personal history." Falk seems to believe the author when he says that he "found in the plays he could level with an audience more easily than he could talk with a friend,"[33] and this remark is also taken seriously by Francis Donahue. In his preface to *The Dramatic World of Tennessee Williams* (1964) Donahue also quotes Williams as saying that "A poet's life is his work and his work is his life," and he implies that his own conversations with the author give him privileged insights into the work. Donahue is yet another Williams scholar who insists on the importance of psychology, ar-guing, for example, that the author's "soft manner . . . masked personal tensions and compulsive feelings which are the mainspring of his art," and that Williams's works are works of "psychic intensity."[34]

With *Tennessee Williams: The Rebellious Puritan* (1961), Nancy M. Tischler emerged as another critic intent on linking playwright to play. In particular, as her title suggests, she focuses on the playwright's struggle with his Puritan heritage. *A Streetcar Named Desire,* then, reflects Williams's own ambivalence toward sex; for, according to Tischler, "he [i.e., Williams] can't decide whether he's for sex or against it," and this is symptomatic of his conflict between rebellion and repression.[35]

In *The Broken World of Tennessee Williams* (1965), Esther M. Jackson, like Tischler, links Williams to the Puritan legacy, but she sees the plays as even more didactic. Jackson sees Williams as attempting to develop "a comprehensive moral structure" and portrays Williams in his work as involved in "an individual search to redeem a shattered universe."[36] A considerable number of other Williams scholars have concentrated on Williams's alleged morality. Arthur Ganz, for example, argues that Williams's morality is "a special one" and that Williams is at his best as a playwright when he is at his most forceful as a moralist. It is also worth noting that even Williams's mother got in on the act of interpreting Williams's plays in terms of morality. In *Remember Me to Tom* (1963), she describes how as a small boy her son, Tom, was found digging and exclaimed, "I'm diggin' to de debbil." She conjectures that in his subsequent work, her son could be seen as filling out this childhood statement by "trying to discover where the devil lies inside all of us."[37]

In an interview with Mike Steen, Anaïs Nin says, "Nowadays even in his everyday life he uses dialogue that's in his plays. . . . To a friend he'll repeat some particular line that he has just written as if not on the printed page but it is coming from him at that moment." Nin insists that "He is now part of his plays and his plays are him, and he is in his plays."[38]

People writing about Williams and his plays in the Seventies persist in drawing connections: especially still in terms of morality. George-Michel Sarotte, for example, sees Tennessee Williams as a "classic psychoanalytic homosexual case history," which inevitably finds its way into the plays. Daniel A. Dervin reads the plays in terms of "subliminal and suggested incest" inextricably connected to the playwright's own experience.[39]

Like many of Williams's early critics, then, Foster Hirsh, in *A Portrait of the Artist: The Plays of Tennessee Williams* (1978), sees Williams as a moralist (albeit a confused one) struggling with puritanical forces. Hirsch sees himself as continuing a tendency on the part of both the public at large and Williams himself to see the author's plays and his life as "intimately connected." "The dramas in fact are written," maintains Hirsch, "in such a way as to compel us to psychoanalyze their author." He sees the playwright as "a reluctant Dionysian, a guilt-ridden reveler," and he sees Williams as using "his own deepest sexual impulses as the base on which to construct complex dramatic characters." For Hirsch, Williams is like "a Southern Gothic

version of Jean Genet. He is a guilty sex-singer, an unliberated bohemian, a hip puritan who nourishes his art with his own tangled sexual
preoccupations." At the same time, insisting on seeing the playwright
in the context of Southern writers, Hirsch argues that "Williams is
absorbed by a romantic vision of the past—the Old South." Hirsch
sees Williams as creating plays out of "neurotic conflicts in his own
personality" and this personality is somehow a self-contained unity.
"Being among the most private and self-enclosed of famous authors,"
says Hirsh, "[Williams] writes in order to exorcise his own demons,
and he is always triumphantly and inescapably himself."[40]

In his highly praised *A Critical Introduction to Twentieth Century
American Drama*, C. W. E. Bigsby follows many other scholars in
arguing that in his work Williams may be seen as struggling against
psychological forces. Bigsby is more comprehensive than most, however, in associating these forces with history: he notes, for example,
the influence on Williams's early work made by the Depression of the
1930s, the second world war, and the advent of the nuclear age. He
also sees Williams as depicting the desperate plight of the lonely and
alienated who, despite the threat of alienation, are able to survive
with dignity. According to Bigsby, like Arthur Miller, Tennessee Williams is concerned with the public or social world's "erosion of private
space" that can lead to the collapse of the individual. "Needing," says
Bigsby, "to believe in the integrity of a resistant self, they [the two
playwrights] shift the threat of collapse onto the form of the play
(*Death of a Salesman* and *Camino Real*) or onto a dramatic symbol
which must stand for that collapse (the unicorn in *The Glass Menagerie*, the dried-up fountain in *Camino Real*, the concentration camp
in *After the Fall*)."[41]

Continuing earlier critics tendency to link playwright and play,
Bigsby affirms the special link between playwright and character.
Thus, when discussing "the tortured, alienated, and vulnerable figures
which he [Williams] places on stage," Bigsby insists that "in some
undeniable sense they are him, if not in the sensational sense that
journalist–reviewers frequently choose to believe."[42] An example of
this would be characters' feelings of self-pity, which, according to
Bigsby, are entangled with Williams's own feelings of self-pity; for
even in Williams's best work "the note of self-pity . . . is never entirely absent."[43]

Although Bigsby's "some undeniable sense" remains undefined; undeniable yet undefined, the way in which Bigsby's attempts to find

the playwright in the plays is clear and is imitable. As an example of the kind of extrapolation to which Bigsby is prone, we might sight this claim concerning Williams's art:

> His art was the communication of a pathologically shy man; his accounts of characters unable to reach one another, or even to convey a sense of the nature and profundity of their need, an expression of his own fear that his plays themselves were an imperfect communication.[44]

These characters unable to reach each other could be found in any number of Williams's plays. In fact, Bigsby's remark fits in nicely with Williams's own remarks about the need for communication that he made in an interview and supported by referring to *The Night of the Iguana*:

> Well the drama in my plays, I think is nearly always people trying to reach each other. In *Night of the Iguana* each one has his separate cubicle, but they meet on the veranda outside the cubicles . . . which is, of course, an allegorical touch of what most people try to do. It's true they're confined within their own skins, or their own cubicles . . . they must try to find a common ground on which they can meet, because the only truly satisfying moments in life are those in which you are in contact. (CN, 86–87)

Williams insists that he needs to communicate, needs to make contact, "a deeper contact than physical with some other human being" (CN, 87). Thus, Bigsby seems to be on safe ground when he links the inability of characters to reach one another with the playwright's fears concerning the difficulty of communication.

Bigsby's tendency to link playwright and play is nowhere more apparent than in his treatment of *Camino Real*. He suggests, for example, that "the 'Terra Incognita' into which Kilroy, the protagonist, moves reflects Williams's own sense of moving in a new direction, going beyond the immediate realities of his own experience, finding a setting other than the claustrophobic Southern town of his youth and a form much looser and less controlled than that of his first plays."[45]

As this kind of speculative link between playwright and work is typical of some recent Williams scholarship, I would like to suggest some links of my own—focusing for now on *Camino Real*.

Camino Real and Williams's "Real" Me

Camino Real can be seen as translating Williams's work experience. In particular, the play exemplifies a number of the playwright's needs:

for example, the need to continue writing, the need for inspiration (especially when progress seems difficult), the need to do something new, and the need to successfully compete with other playwrights.

"Maybe I am a machine," says Williams, "a typist. A compulsive typist and a compulsive writer. But that's my life, and what in these memoirs is mostly the barest periphery of that which is my intense life, for my intense life is my work" (MS, 84–85). I feel the presence of this "compulsive" worker in some of the early lines from the beginning of *Camino Real*. Thus when Don Quixote says, "The time for retreat never comes!" (CR, 5), this could mean the playwright must go on, continue writing, not rest on his laurels. "You should remember," says Williams, "that you are always competing with your earlier work. You have to. In my particular case, they all say, Oh, that *Glass Menagerie*! until you almost begin to hate it. Because you know that you have been working all the time since. And it's not quite possible that you haven't created something since then" (CN, 122). Williams may, to some extent, have "to hock his sweet used-to-be in order to finance his present situation" (CR, 32), in other words, live off the enormous gains, both in material wealth and popularity, which he accrued from the success of *The Glass Menagerie* and *A Streetcar Named Desire*: "Used to be," says The Baron, "is the past tense, meaning useless" (CR, 37). The playwright's success or failure, then, is always dependent on what he is doing right now.

The idea of moving from what one has done in the past (the familiar) to what one needs to do now (the unknown) may be reflected in the epigraph to *Camino Real*, which Williams takes from Dante: "In the middle of the journey of our life I came to myself in a dark wood where the straight way was lost" (Epigraph taken from Dante's *Inferno*, Canto 1; translator unnamed). In Block Three, the Gypsy asks, through her loudspeaker, "Do you wish that things could be *straight* and simple again as they were in your childhood?" (emphasis added; CR, 28). The lines from Dante may be linked to the playwright's desire to attempt something new, to find a new "way" to form a play (Notice that the word *camino* in Spanish also means "way.") This fits in with Bigsby's notion about finding a form that is much looser.

There is always a danger that the play will be laughed at—the critics will ridicule it, audiences will hate it and will storm out of the theater, demanding their money back. In fact, this is precisely what happened to the first run of *Camino Real*. In his foreword to the published text of the play Williams describes the situation:

At each performance a number of people have stamped out of the auditorium, with little regard for those whom they had to crawl over . . . and there have been sibilant noises on the way out and demands for money back if the cashier was foolish enough to remain in his box." (CR, vii)

Doubtless, many of the people walking out of those first performances of *Camino Real* felt displeased with the playwright. Perhaps they failed to see that the play is a kind of a parody of the playwright's efforts. When Esmeralda urges Kilroy, "Be Champ again! Contend in the contest! Compete in the competition!" (CR, 105), this could be advice for the formerly extremely successful playwright. Perhaps the humiliation experienced by Kilroy who is made to dress up as a clown, to wear "the Patsy outfit—the red fright wig, the big crimson nose that lights up and has horn-rimmed glasses attached, a pair of clown pants that have a huge footprint on the seat" (CR, 48–49) is, potentially, at least, the humiliation of the playwright.

Although apparently not much of an actor, Williams once acted in one of his own plays. It was an off-Broadway production of *Small Craft Warnings*. During an interval, he came out of a side door and screamed at two members of the audience who were arguing in the aisle: "We're giving our hearts to you."[46] There is the suggestion that for Williams, the act of theater is not mere exploitation of an audience—its presence sustaining a vital selfish need of his own—but it is an act of love. Kilroy offers to "hustle [his] heart on this street" (CR, 37). With each performance, the playwright, like Kilroy can be seen as offering to hustle his own heart on the street. Hustling may involve a certain amount of fraud or deception; the purpose of it is to make money. Is this what the playwright is doing—bringing people into the theater, making money out of them—the more people, the more money; the more money, the better? Whenever the curtain goes up and the play begins, however, he may be putting himself on the line.

In *The Kindness of Strangers: The Life of Tennessee Williams*, Donald Spoto quotes a remark that Williams made to José Quintero following the initial audience's hostile reactions to *Camino Real*: "Well, I don't think they are really taking the play to their hearts, would you say?"[47] and Spoto goes on to suggest that the play dramatizes Williams's own fears as a middle-aged poet whose "vocation," says Spoto, "is to influence the heart." Spoto suggests that "He ought to purify it [the heart] and lift it above its ordinary level. But at the same time there is the fear that his vocation has been lost in the frenzy of celebrity."[48]

Indeed, it is possible to argue that with every production of one of his plays, Williams offers his heart to the audience. During the early stages of production of the play, *The Seven Descents of Myrtle*, Estelle Parsons was very much affected by the presence of Tennessee Williams, and particularly by his laughter. She commented afterward to Mike Steen, "Sometimes it would be nice to hear him laugh and other times I would wonder what he was laughing at. . . . I felt that he seemed very naked. . . . You meet few people even in the theater who are not awfully well covered up in social circumstances. But Tennessee doesn't seem to be. He just puts his heart right out on the line the whole time."[49] Lord Byron explains how at Shelley's dramatic cremation on the beach at Viareggio, Shelley's friend Trelawney reached into the flames and pulled the heart out of the burning corpse. "I thought it was a disgusting thing to do," says Byron, "to snatch a man's heart from his body! What can one man do with another man's heart?" (CR, 76). This question is answered very graphically by Jacques:

> *Jacques [passionately].* He can do this with it!
> [*He seizes a loaf of bread on his table, and descends from the terrace.*]
> He can twist it like this!
> [*He twists the loaf.*]
> He can tear it like this!
> [*He tears the loaf in two.*]
> He can crush it under his feet!
> [*He drops the bread and stamps on it.*]
> And kick it away—like this!
> [*He kicks the bread off the terrace. . . .*]

(CR, 76)

Any one who knew Williams well can tell you how devastated he was by unfavorable reviews of his work. He has admitted that he wants an audience's approval: "Of course, I want their approval, I want their understanding and their empathy" (MS, xvii).

We can also extract from *Camino Real,* the idea that Williams is competitive. Williams may be like the Don Quixote of *Camino Real* who says, "The time for retreat never comes!" (CR, 5), for the playwright must continue writing, continue competing not just with himself, but with other playwrights. When Esmeralda urges Kilroy, "Be Champ again! Contend in the contest! Compete in the competition!" (CR, 105), this could be advice for Williams himself, a playwright who was no longer enjoying the success that came his way as a result of his earlier work. "You should remember," says Williams, "that you are always competing with your earlier work. You have to. In my particular case, they all say, Oh, that *Glass Menagerie!* until you al-most begin to hate it. Because you know that you have been working all the time since. And it's not quite possible that you haven't created something since then" (CN, 122).

In fact, Williams has argued that he does not compete with other playwrights. "I don't compete with Eugene O'Neill or anyone else," declares Williams, "My work is totally in its own category" (CN, 341). Nevertheless, in interviews he often compares playwrights as if there were a competition, saying for example that Harold Pinter is "the greatest living contemporary playwright" and that Tom Stoppard is not a playwright at all: "I find him a charlatan. He's not funny. He's an intellectual poseur. I hate to say bad things about a fellow playwright—but this man's not in my opinion a playwright" (CN, 319). The tone and the emphasis suggests to me that he is enjoying saying these things. Notice that he also says that "O'Neill is not as good a playwright as for instance, Albee" (CN, 341), and earlier he claimed that Edward Albee was "indisputably the best present-day American playwright" (CN, 319). Surely, the choice of the term *pres-ent-day* leaves open the possibility that he himself was once the best American playwright. It is interesting to put his comments on O'Neill alongside Rader's suggestion following the account he gives of how Williams once asked him to frame a signed photograph that he had received from Eugene O'Neill. According to Rader, O'Neill never actually sent his photograph to Williams; in other words, this was another fiction invented by Williams. Rader believes the writing on the portrait to have been penned by Williams's own hand. Rader claims that "Williams considered the author of *Long Day's Journey Into Night* to be his only competitor in the pantheon of American playwrights. He thought that O'Neill was, after himself, the nation's greatest playwright." Rader presents a strong case to suggest that Williams did indeed see himself as competing with O'Neill, and that he did resent repeatedly being referred to as "the greatest American playwright since that great O'Neill" (TCH, 254–56).

In Block 2, the Survivor desperately searches for water, but he is told *"la Fuente esta seca!"* (CR, 14). As the survivor needs water, the playwright needs inspiration, a flow of inspiration. At times he may feel that it is hard to continue. Through her loudspeaker, the Gypsy asks,

> Have you arrived at a point on the Camino Real where the walls converge not in the distance but right in front of your nose? Does further progress seem impossible to you? Are you afraid of nothing at all? Afraid of your heartbeat? Or the eyes of strangers? (CR, 28)

The playwright must overcome any fear that he may have of these eyes, the eyes of audiences, and he must keep writing. It may even be a question of his survival. The playwright wants to be "here," that is to say, he wants somehow to exist in the theater or in his written play; but in *Camino Real* even the characters question their existence. Indeed, Bigsby quotes Marguerite in *Camino Real*:

> What are we sure of? Not even of our existence, dear comforting friend! And whom can we ask the question that torments us? "What is this place?" "Where are we?"—a fat old man gives sly hints that only bewilder us more, a fake of a Gypsy squinting at cards and tea-leaves. What else are we offered? The never-broken procession of little events that assure us that we and strangers about us are still going on! . . . We hear the Streetcleaners' piping not far away. So, now and then, although we've wounded each other time and time again—we stretch out hands to each other in the dark that we can't escape from—we huddle together for some dim-communal comfort. . . . Something, yes, something . . . delicate, unreal, bloodless! (CR, 96–97)

Bigsby describes this as a "deconstructive vision" and adds that "the sense of dislocation of logic and continuity is a major force in Williams's work."[50] Bigsby, however, fails to note that this "deconstructive vision" also renders problematic the straightforward existence of the author. The "presence" of the author here or anywhere else in Williams's plays is a supposition (or superstition?) in need of rigorous examination. The characters, unsure of their own existence, may be "self-regarding fictions,"[51] but the author too may be only a "self-regarding fiction." It is possible to see Williams as "lonely," as "frightened," as stretching out his hands to audiences, and as hoping to provide or share with them "some dim-communal comfort." Is this the "real" Williams though, or is this one as "unreal," as "bloodless," as the love of which Marguerite speaks?

In the title of the play, *Camino Real,* the whole notion of the "real" is recognized as problematic. If we know Spanish, we will realize that in Spanish *real* can mean "royal" as well as "real." In the opening scene, Sancho reads instructions from a torn parchment: "Continue until you come to the square of a walled town which is the end of

the Camino Real and the beginning of the Camino Real. Halt there
. . . and turn back, Traveler, for the spring of humanity has gone
dry in this place and—" (Williams's emphasis; CR, 5). There is the
suggestion here of a point of transition, a possibility of transgression,
a movement from the "royal" to the "real." Perhaps the play that
follows takes place at this junction between the two, between the
"royal" and the "real," but there is a question about whether one can
ever actually get to the "real." In his foreword to the play, Williams
uses a familiar metaphor to explain the fact that members of the audience left the theater before the end of the first performance:

> A cage represents security as well as confinement to a bird that has grown
> used to being in it; and when a theatrical work kicks over the traces
> with such apparent insouciance, security seems challenged and, instead of
> participating in its sense of freedom, one out of a certain number of play-
> goers will rush back out to the more accustomed implausibility of the
> street. (CR, ix)[52]

This is another example of the questioning of the "real." Which is
more real, play or street outside? If the play is in some sense unreal,
how can the "real" playwright be present in it? Notice also that in
the epigraph, it is "In the middle of the journey of our life" that "I
came to myself" (emphasis added), as if through the writing of the
play, the playwright comes to know his authentic self, a "real" self
that spectators or readers of the play can also come to know.

Can we really believe that an author can be, in Hirsch's words,
"always triumphantly and inescapably himself"?[53] Isn't that self always changing? And even if an author believes that he or she has
come to know himself or herself, can a biographer come to this same
awareness? The sustaining illusion for the biographer is that one can
get access to this "real" self, what many seem to think of as "a living
and breathing presence."[54]

Even if we are beginning to realize, however, that the idea of digging
deep and finding the "real Me" is somewhat naive, we should not try
to take anything away from the work of the biographers who frequently have noble intentions, have undertaken copious research, and
have offered us loving portraits of their subjects. Indeed, Edel may be
right when he claims that most biographies are written in affection
and love.[55]

The traditional way of linking author and work used by Bigsby and
which I have adopted to some extent here, however, needs to be

rethought. Bigsby's study of Williams, like most studies that attempt to connect authors with their works, is based largely on unstated and unexamined suppositions. In an age when dichotomies, like that between world of theater and world outside, are being blown asunder, the presumed connection between author and work needs to be reexamined. In particular, we should try to find out what is left of the biographical subject in the context of postmodernism.

2

Literary Biography Turns to Intertextuality and the Proper Name

For if, through a twisted dialectic, the Text, destroyer of all subject, contains a subject to love, that subject is dispersed, somewhat like the ashes we strew into the wind after death.

—Roland Barthes

The subject of writing does not exist if we mean by that some sovereign solitude of the author. The subject of writing is a system of relations . . .

—Jacques Derrida

Literary biography, then, lives off the impossibility of its own project. The search for the "real" author in the author's work is inevitably problematic, and biography has a problem living up to the idea that it can unearth, produce, create, or recreate such an entity. Nevertheless, as James Clifford observes, "Biography, relying on little theoretical sophistication . . . manages with surprising consistency to make us believe in the existence of a self."[1] At the same time as inviting us to question what he calls "the myth of personal coherence," however, Clifford also raises the possibility of a different kind of biography, one which would substitute "openness and discontinuity" for "closure and progress toward individuality."[2]

Clifford borrows the phrase "hanging up looking glasses at odd corners" from Virginia Woolf who had suggested that biography could "enlarge its scope" by adopting various, not always obvious, perspectives. A diversity of approaches to biography in Woolf's opinion would "bring out, not a risk of confusion, but a richer unity."[3] It is by no means clear, though, how this "unity" could be achieved. Indeed, the notion of unity, as in, for example, totalized meaning or absolutely coherent individuality, seems to me to be irreconcilable with postmodernism or any postmodernist conception of the bio-graphical subject. Clifford himself does not emphasize unity, and so his notion of a more open and discontinuous approach to biography has a more postmodern ring to it. He leaves it largely to others though to see how his idea could work in practice.

I would argue that a more open and discontinuous approach to biography had in fact been pervasive in France for some time before Clifford's 1978 essay appeared. In fact, Clifford hints at this when he cites Camus' claim that "seen from the outside they [lives] form a whole. While our life, seen from inside, is all bits and pieces."[4] In their writing, postmodernists like Roland Barthes and Jacques Derrida have frequently resorted to fragments and have tended to resist totaliz-ing projects in favor of "bits and pieces." In particular, Barthes, for example, recognizes that by imposing order on a work the literary critic distorts the work's reality. Similarly in the insistence on order the biographer can be seen as inevitably distorting the subject's life.

Many readers of Barthes' work may have failed to see to what extent the biographical construction of authorship is his subject. His apparent rejection of a criticism that attempts to explain a literary work in terms of an "elsewhere" of literature includes a rejection of not only explanation in terms of historical moment, but also in terms of the emotions or intentions experienced by the author. In *Criticism and Truth*, Barthes proposes a literary science that will do away with the idea of an author as source and guarantor of the meaning of the work. Barthes argues that the real origins of a work are mythological and not to be found in authorial intention:

> We are generally inclined, at least today, to believe that the author can lay claim to the meaning of his work and can himself make that its legal meaning; from this notion flows the unreasonable interrogation directed by the critic at the dead writer, at his life, at the traces of his intentions, so that he himself can guarantee the meaning of his work: people want at all costs to make the dead author or a substitute for him, speak. Such substitutes may be his historical period, the genre, the vocabulary, in a word everything that is contemporary with the author.[5]

Barthes urges us to "free the work from the constraints of intention" and to "rediscover the mythological tremblings of meaning" (CT, 77). *Criticism and Truth* is in part a response to an attack made on Barthes by Raymond Picard, who had maintained that language could be transparent and that literal meanings were possible—accessible to both author and critic. Barthes, on the other hand, emphasizes the complexity or "depth" of language, the idea that language is problem-atic for both author and critic. "A writer is someone," says Barthes, "for whom language constitutes a problem, who is aware of the depth of language, not its instrumentality or its beauty" (CT, 64). "Formerly separated by the worn-out myth of the '*superb creator and the humble servant, both necessary, each in his place, etc.*', the writer and the critic come together, working on the same difficult tasks and faced with the same object: language" (Barthes' emphasis; CT, 64). Barthes then places a fresh emphasis on the activity of the reader, and it becomes difficult to disassociate the text from the reader's working with the text.

In their introduction to a recent collection of essays stemming from a conference held at the University of East Anglia, entitled appropri-ately *The Troubled Face of Biography,* E. Homberger and J. Charmley refer their readers to Barthes' more celebrated 1968 article, "The Death of the Author," in which Barthes expands on what he had to say in *Criticism and Truth* about the inappropriateness of turning to the author for explanations. Homberger and Charmley cite this passage,

> The image of literature to be found in ordinary culture is tyrannically centered on the author, his person, his life, his tastes, his passions, while criticism still consists for the most part in saying that Baudelaire's work is the failure of Baudelaire the man, Van Gogh his madness, Tchaikovsky's his vice. The *explanation* of a work is always sought in the man or woman who produced it, as if it were always in the end, through the more or less transparent allegory of fiction, the voice of a single person, the *author* "confiding" in us. (Barthes' emphasis; IMT, 143)

Homberger and Charmley suggest that although in 1968 Barthes' scorn for a simplistic belief in "confiding" authors may have been "a polemical overstatement," it has now become "entrenched academic dogma."[6] Surely, however, explanations of works continue to be sought in the author. If the author is still alive someone can interview the author and ask what (s)he meant or what (s)he intended. In addi-tion to interviewing the author or reading interviews with the author, we may be able to scour his or her autobiography for the creator's privileged insights into the work. Finding no explicit statements by the author, we can produce our own clever interpretations and pat ourselves on the back when we feel we know the author well enough to think that we have accurately read his or her mind.

Many students believe that any difficulties they have with a text can be explained away by the author's simply telling them what (s)he was trying to say or, as many students in Freshmen English classes put it, "the point that the author was trying to get across." Although most people seem to assume that the point will be ethical, for Barthes the complexity of language precludes the possibility of the "real" writer invoking a univocal ethical imperative. There is no single certain meaning to be found. Literary language is of necessity always symbolic: writing "sets up ambiguities, not a meaning" (CT, 72). The only certainty is that writing takes the form of language. According to Susan Sontag, "Barthes understood . . . that literature is first of all, last of all, language. It is language that is everything."[7] Thus for Barthes, writing does not "present" or "constitute" the author: "it is language which speaks, not the author; to write is, through a prerequisite impersonality . . . to reach that point where only language acts, 'performs,' and not 'me'" (IMT, 143).

Indeed Homberger and Charmley may be write in seeing Barthes as indulging in "polemical overstatement," for his own position regarding the position of the author seems hardly consistent unless he wants to deny that he himself is speaking as he writes. Sontag suggests Valéry's dictum concerning the author as underlying Barthes' rejection of the author. "The work," Valéry insists, "should not give the person it affects anything that can be reduced to an idea of the author's person and thinking."[8] As Sontag points out though, "this commitment to impersonality does not preclude the avowal of the self; it is only another variation on the project of self-examination, the noblest project of French literature."[9] In practice then "most of Barthes' writing is precisely devoted to personal singularity."[10]

In *Sade/Fourier/Loyola*, Barthes again makes it clear that the author of whom he speaks does not correspond to our traditional conception of the author: "The author who returns," declares Barthes, "is not the one identified by our institutions [history, and courses in literature, philosophy, and church discourse]; he is not even the biographical hero." "The author," says Barthes, "who leaves his text and comes into our life has no unity; he is a mere plural of 'charms,' the site of a few tenuous details . . . he is not a (civil, moral) person, he is a body."[11] Details like Sade's white muff, Fourier's flower pots, Loyola's "beautiful eyes, always a little filled with tears" (SFL, 8), Barthes labels "biographemes." He goes on to convey a sense of wonder at the transmission of biographemes:

> Were I a writer, and dead, how I would love it if my life through the pains of some friendly and detached biographer, were to reduce itself to a few details, a few preferences, a few inflections, let us say: to "biogra-phemes" whose distinction and mobility might go beyond any fate and come to touch, like Epicurean atoms, some future body, destined to the same dispersion. (SFL, 9)

Despite the movement toward the openness of which Clifford would speak several years later, Barthes then seems to retain the notion of an author as a body capable of reaching out to and touching another body (a reader/writer). It is possible, then, for us to live with authors by allowing "the fragments of an intelligible ['formulae'] that emanate from a text we admire" to enter our daily lives (SFL, 7). Thus, the phrase, "The Death of the Author" is, indeed, polemical, but the phrase does not signify the end of the biographical subject; it signifies a rethinking of the biographical subject.

Despite his obvious grounding in formalism and structuralism, even the title of his book, *Sade/Fourier/Loyola,* draws attention to authors and suggests that Barthes is by no means prepared to give up on the author. Indeed, in his conception of bodies touching (author and reader), there is a hint of the Romanticism demonstrated by some of the more traditional biographical theorists. Barthes, however, moves away from questions of an author's social responsibility and argues that "There are those who believe they can with assurance discuss the site of this responsibility: it would be the author, inserting that author into his history, his class. But another site remains enigmatic, escapes for the time being any illumination: the site of the reading" (SFL, 9–10). For readers this site, which Barthes suggests is traversed by author and work (SFL, 176), will be different depending on readers' own capacity or inclination to work or play.

In "Theory of the Text," rather than seeing the text as a product, Barthes sees the text as a productivity, as "the very theater of a production where the producer and the reader of a text meet" (TT, 36). The reader is allowed to invent "ludic meanings, even if the inventor of the text had not foreseen them, and even if it was histori-cally impossible for him to see them: the signifier belongs to every-body" (TT, 37). Barthes sees signification as happening on the level of product—the text as product (the text as finished closed entity) and replaces this term with the term *signifiance,* which suggests the text actively at work within the reader. He sees the text as "perpetual productions through which the subject continues to struggle; this subject is no doubt that of the author, but also that of the reader" (TT, 42). This is a far cry from New Criticism where the reader's engagement with a text is suppressed in the interest of preserving the text's autonomy. Although Barthes' theory may appear to have something in common with reader-response criticism (as practiced, for example, by Norman Holland), Barthes is not interested in individual reader's psychological makeup. Nevertheless, Barthes does emphasize the reader and many Anglo-Saxon commentators seem very disturbed because the reader is given such an active role. Commentators are worried that now anything goes. They are worried that critics will now be able to say "just anything at all" (CT, 80). They seem to fear that the death of the author means an end to biographical criticism, heralding instead the advent of endlessly playful readers' games and a rush of signifiers permanently divorced from any signifieds. Barthes admits that "it is henceforth less a question of explaining or even describing, than of entering into the play of the signifiers." Furthermore, unlike criticism that seeks the meaning of a work, the kind of textual analysis advocated and practiced by Barthes, "impugns the idea of a final signified" (TT, 43).[12]

The idea of entering into the play of signifiers is in keeping with postmodernism's tendency to revel in play. If we look back to the conference at East Anglia, we find what could be regarded as a widespread Francophobia or, at least, a prevailing resistance to Continental theory. Thus, in "How I Fell into Biography," Michael Holroyd sees the author as being replaced by the team of reader and critic. "French critics," he says, "have gone so far as to use Sartre's failure to complete his work on Flaubert to reinforce their banishment of literary biography" and goes on to suggest, "No wonder the biographer has been resistant to poststructuralism and the theory of deconstruction."[13] In the essay that closes the volume, "The Telling Life: Some Thoughts on Literary Biography" Malcolm Bradbury goes to absurd lengths to emphasize that authors are not only "real" people but are also the sources of their work:

> they [authors] have a visibility, even a certain fame, and they are unquestionably there; we can see them, touch them if we are lucky, and have them put their own signatures to their books in the bookstores. They

gesture to us from our TV screens . . . occasionally even discussing their own work. They have lives and wives and lovers and mistresses, and from time to time they go to jail, or go to France, or win a famous prize or a state accolade. . . . From all they say and do it seems evident that it was they, and not writing in general, that conceived and developed and pro-duced their books, that the images and preoccupations derived in some fashion from their own experience.[14]

Surely, no one is denying that authors are "real" people or that they conceive, develop, and produce books. What Barthes is questioning is the nature of the link between authors and their books. Because writers do not create out of nothing there is always linkage between one text and other texts, and this raises questions about originality. In "The Death of the Author," Barthes argues that "writing is the destruction of every voice, of every point of origin" (IMT, 142), and he credits Mallarmé with foreseeing

the necessity to substitute language itself for the person who until then had been supposed to be its owner. For him, for us too, it is language which speaks, not the author; to write is through a prerequisite impersonality . . . to reach that point where only language acts, "performs," and not "me." (IMT, 143)

As we have seen, however, this does not mean that there is no author. Barthes is simply proposing a different way of looking at the author. As we study a text we can never be sure what authors are express-ing—what sense they are making of their own experience—but we can look for author's inscriptions in an intertextual network.

In "The Death of the Author," Barthes argues, "We know now that a text is not a line of words releasing a single 'theological meaning' (the message of the Author-God) but a multidimensional space in which a variety of writings, none of them original, blend and clash" (IMT, 146). It is important to distinguish between the word "work" and the word "text." In "From Work to Text," he suggests, "The author is reputed the father and the owner of the work: literary sci-ence teaches respect for the manuscript and the author's declared intentions" (IMT, 160).[15] In moving from work to text, Barthes moves from signification to *signifiance,* from work as intentional communica-tion to text as active process. Thus, Barthes goes on to introduce the notion of the intertext, arguing that the text

can be read without the guarantee of its father, the restitution of the inter-text paradoxically abolishing any legacy. It is not that the Author may not

"come back" in the Text, in his text, but he then does so as a "guest." If
he is a novelist, he is inscribed in the novel like one of his characters,
figured in the carpet; no longer privileged, paternal, aletheological, his
inscription is ludic. He becomes, as it were, a paper-author: his life is no
longer the origin of his fictions but a fiction contributing to his work, there
is a reversion of the work onto the life . . . it is the work of Proust, of
Genet which allows their lives to be read as a text. (IMT, 161)

Had there been no work of course, who would be interested in the
lives of Proust or Genet—or Williams? Given that they have written
the works, though, how can their lives be read as anything else but
text? While not denying that "real" authors exist, Barthes' thinking
is to some extent in line with some of the Anglo-Saxon/American
biography theorists, like James Clifford, who were beginning to doubt
the existence of a knowable coherent self. The difference, however,
between Barthes and those theorists who although they acknowledge
the impossibility of their own project, continue to practice that project
in traditional ways is that Barthes offers an alternative approach:
examining an author's inscription—which is "ludic"—in an intertextual network. Rather than looking for the meaning or meanings to be
found in a work the postmodernist biographer influenced by Barthes
is much more concerned with the intertextual resonance. Furthermore, like many of his or her predecessors the postmodernist biographer is suspicious of facts and comes to think more in terms of
relationships.

We return later to the question of intertextuality, but first we
acknowledge that the notion of the subject as not given but having
to be constructed, invented, has been kicking around at least since
Nietzsche. It seems to be especially in contemporary writing on the
autobiographical subject that the view that the subject is created by
and in language has received most attention. In 1979, Paul de Man
was insisting that "the 'moments' in an autobiographical work are not
'located in a history,' but are the 'manifestation . . . of a linguistic
structure.'"[16] Paul L. Jay sees Barthes (along with Paul Valéry) as
redefining rather than dismissing the biographical self. The life is "not
separate from the time of writing, but constituted in and by it." Examining *Roland Barthes by Roland Barthes*, "Barthes's text," says Jay,
"constitutes a denial of the 'fiction' of the subject as anything other
than a creation of human consciousness and human language," and
the subject, the "self," turns out to be "shattered, scattered, decent-
ered, and—at least in a text—always a 'fiction.'"[17] "I am not contradic-

tory," says Barthes, "I am dispersed" (BB, 143). From Barthes' work, then, it is possible to see a new vision of the self emerging as "heaped together" from "dispersed fragments."[18]

Of course, Barthes was not the first to use the term *intertextuality*. Drawing on the work of Bakhtin for the idea, Julia Kristeva was responsible for coining the term *intertextuality*. She used it to describe the way in which "every text is constructed as a mosaic of citations, every text is an absorption and transformation of another text."[19] Barthes, then, employs the term *intertext*: "any text is an intertext; other texts are present in it, at varying levels, in more or less recogniz-able forms. . . . Any text is a new tissue of past citations" (TT, 39). Etymologically the word "text" comes from the Latin *textus* meaning fabric and *texere* to weave; so Barthes' term *tissue* is very appropriate, suggesting an interwoven intricate network.

J. P. Plottel and H. Charney suggest that "intertextuality is the recognition of a frame, a context that allows the reader to make sense out of what he or she might otherwise perceive as senseless."[20] Al-though this may be the case, Barthes would argue that meaning will always be equivocal and that texts always subject to further interpre-tations. "In the multiplicity of writing, he says, "everything is to be *disentangled*, nothing *deciphered*; the structure can be followed . . . but there is nothing beneath: the space of writing is to be ranged over, not pierced; writing ceaselessly posits meaning, ceaselessly to evaporate it, carrying out a systematic exemption of meaning" (Barthes' emphasis; IMT, 147). Thus, intertextuality may not enable us to make more sense. Indeed, as Barthes points out, intertextuality may be regarded as "a little machine for making war against philologi-cal law, the tyranny of correct meaning."[21] Those, like Plottel and Charney, who insist that intertextuality makes texts more meaningful are still operating under the assumptions of a criticism that assumes that the goal of the critic is to seek the meaning or meanings of the work. To replace that kind of criticism, Barthes proposes textual analy-sis; whereas the old approach emphasizes signification, Barthes' tex-tual analysis proposes *signifiance*, which "unlike signification cannot be reduced to communication, to representation, to expression." (TT, 38). Furthermore, Barthes' textual analysis resists the notion that the work has to be "attached to, appropriated by, the . . . person of an author who would be its father." "To the metaphor of filiation, of organic 'development,'" says Barthes, "textual analysis prefers the metaphor of the network, of the intertext, of an overdetermined plural field" (TT, 43). Again, this is the movement from work to text, from work as involving a process of filiation to text as "the substance of a connection."[22]

It is important to distinguish the intertextual approach from the kind of approach practiced, for example, by Harold Bloom who believes that poets are involved in a kind of oedipal struggle for power as they attempt to separate themselves from precursor poets. In rewriting the family romance of poets, Bloom implies that the later poet, is, at some level, aware of the precursor's work, for the later poet is "stationing [his poem] in relation to the parent-poem."[23] Rather than writing within a space of intertextual anonymity, the author for Bloom is involved in an interpersonal struggle, and this accounts for the anxiety.

Following Roland Barthes' lead, however, the kind of approach that I am suggesting gets away from influence study. Barthes does not seem to me to delve into the life of an author to find out what he or she has read and, therefore, what he or she may be borrowing or stealing from—this would be of interest to the traditional biographer as it would to Harold Bloom. Instead, Barthes implies that like him, we should be sensitive to intertextuality. The biographical self is indeed dispersed—between and among a literary text, its pre-texts, and any other text by or about the author. This does not mean that intertextuality or *signifiance* have always to replace the author or signification. Barthes is not trying to nullify the achievements of traditional criticism and literary history.

*   *   *

Like Roland Barthes, Jacques Derrida is concerned with intertextuality and he notes that the word "text" is connected with "textile" and hence the idea of interweaving *(enchainment)*: "This interweaving, this textile," says Derrida, "is the *text* produced only in the transformation of another text."[24] Also like Barthes, Derrida has been determined to show ways of approaching texts that do not see texts as productions and the critic's task as simply involving deciphering texts' meanings. Instead, Derrida talks about the freeplay *(jeu)* of the text, and he has consequently been reproached for failing to recognize that texts have decidable meanings. One of Derrida's detractors, G. B. Madison, for example, interprets Derrida as saying that "meaning is nothing other than the ephemeral play of language itself; it refers only to itself, in an endless, disseminating deferral of any definite refer-

ent."[25] Madison's claim is based in large measure on Derrida's bold
assertion in *Of Grammatology* that "There is nothing outside of the
text [there is no outside-text; *il n' y a pas de hors-texte*],[26] which
leads Madison to conclude that "for Derrida there is no exit from the
labyrinth of a text, no finished, decidable meaning, merely an endless
play of signifiers."[27]

In "Deconstruction and Meaning: The Textuality Game," E. Warwick Slinn argues that *"il n' y a pas de hors-texte"* should not be
translated as "nothing but the text" but, as is more usually the case,
as "no outside the text" or "no outside text." "We are not to be
confined to 'text,'" says Slinn, "whatever it happens to be, in a manner
resembling new critical isolation of the text as verbal icon, but are to
confront the proposition that there is nothing outside textuality, no
referent that is not already part of a system of signification."[28] This
is clearly not the same as interpreting Derrida as simply pointing to
"an endless play of signifiers." In the pages that follow I regard the
author as not flesh and blood but, indeed, as "part of a system of
signification," as a sign, in other words, whose meaning is to be derived from its relation to other signs in the intertextual network.

Early on in his career on the subject of allusion, which is fundamental of course to an understanding of intertextuality, Derrida suggests,
realistically but somewhat cynically, that "one can never know what
the allusion alludes to, unless it is to itself in the process of alluding. . . ."[29] "As its name indicates," says Derrida, "allusion *plays*. But
that this play should in the last instance be independent of truth does
not mean that it is false, an error, appearance, or illusion" (Derrida's
emphasis; DS, 219).[30] Derrida is determined to deny that play precludes sense. I return to this fundamentally important notion in chapter 3.

Despite Barthes' polemic in "Death of the Author," I have argued
that the author continues to exist for Barthes, existing through inscription in an intertextual network. Similarly, I suggest that the author
continues to exist for Derrida. In *Signéponge/Signsponge,* Derrida
talks about "that death or omission of the author of which, as is
certainly the case, too much of a case has been made,"[31] and in working
through the textualizing of the author's proper name (Francis Ponge),
Derrida may be seen as reacting to the structuralists and formalists'
attempt to banish the author from the scene of writing. The author
continues to exist for Derrida through the play of the proper name,
which I suggest is also inseparable from the intertextual network.

Common sense, if there is still such a thing, tells us that it makes no sense to make sense of proper names. Many years ago, in fact, J. S. Mill argued that "proper names do not have senses, they are meaning-less marks, they have denotation but not connotation."[32] In the twen-tieth century, however, John Searle has been bold enough to maintain that there is some connection between the proper name and the object to which it refers:

> My answer, then, to the question, "Do proper names have senses?"—if this asks whether or not proper names are used to describe or specify characteristics of objects—is "No". But if it asks whether or not proper names are logically connected with characteristics of the object to which they refer, the answer is "Yes, in a loose sort of way."[33]

Searle seems to employ this phrase "loose sort of way" because the specific nature of the connections need not be specified. Searle main-tains that it is enough to have, for example, some "essential and estab-lished facts about Aristotle" for us to be able to say "This is Aristotle."[34] He argues that proper names are convenient because with them "we can refer publicly to objects without being forced to raise issues and come to an agreement as to which descriptive characteris-tics exactly constitute the identity of the object."[35]

Another alternative to Mill's position may be found in the work of Derrida. First, Derrida argues that "the proper name . . . should not have meaning and should spend itself in immediate reference." Here Derrida may seem to be agreeing with Mill, but his use of "should" implies that what "should" be the case may, in fact, not be the case at all. A person's name should offer no description of the person to which it refers and have no other reference than that person. "But," Derrida continues, "the chance or the misery of its [i.e., the proper name's] arbitrary character . . . is that its inscription in language al-ways affects it with a potential for meaning." (S/S, 118). As the name becomes meaningful, Derrida suggests that "it starts to re-enter the framework of a general science that governs the effects of the *alea*" (S/S, 120).

Christopher Norris, a great admirer of the Derridean project, ex-plains that "he [Derrida] insists on paying the most scrupulous atten-tion to the way in which proper names *signify,* or take on attributes of (seemingly improper) sense. Expressed in terms of his favorite dis-tinction, it may be the case that proper names are de jure protected from semantic drift, but this protection is undermined by the evident (de facto) possibility of proving otherwise." Norris sees "slippage from naming to signification" as "a process let loose within language by the mere fact that names cannot always be prevented from taking on lexical attributes."[36]

As well as their ability to signify, the other important point about proper names for Derrida, is that through the author's proper name, he or she does not simply exist as something outside of his or her text; for the name may be viewed as a part of the text, caught up in textual play or intertextuality. Thus, through the proper name, and I argue that it is not necessarily his or her own name, the author becomes a part of the intertextual network. Derrida's work on the proper name, then, may be regarded as a supplement, a "dangerous supplement," to Barthes' model of intertextuality.

One must seriously question Malcolm Bradbury's reading of Derrida's *Signéponge/Signsponge* as an anti-biography[37] because instead of eliminating the author (Ponge), Derrida reinscribes the author by means of the play of his proper name. In fact, far from dismissing the biographical project, Derrida himself has read works as autobiographical and is on record as admitting that "Everything I write is terribly autobiographical."[38] I believe that paying serious attention to intertextuality and the proper name opens up new possibilities for both reading and writing and can lead to the emergence of a different kind of biography.

*   *   *

Into and Out of *Battle of Angels*

A tree sprang up. O sheer transcendency!
O Orpheus sings! O tall tree in the ear!
And all was still. Yet even in that silence
a new beginning, hint, and change appeared.
                              —Rainer Maria Rilke[39]

Appearing in 1940, *Battle of Angels,* Williams's first full-length play to be given a professional production, was later rewritten and published as *Orpheus Descending* in 1957.[40] The retitling of the play as *Orpheus Descending* automatically connects the play to all pre-texts that concern the legend of Orpheus. As a musician, Valentine Xavier, who plays a guitar in *Orpheus Descending,* is clearly linked to Orpheus, the seductive player of the magic lyre. Like Orpheus, Val is the object of much female yearning. In Virgil's "Georgic IV," Orpheus "angered the Thracian maids whose kiss he scorned."[41] In Ovid's *Metamorphoses,* Book X, "many a woman burned with passion for / a bard."[42] Both Val and Orpheus, however, need solitude and tend to hold themselves aloof from women. Near the end of *Battle of Angels,* Val tells Myra that were she to go with him to the desert, she "would make it too crowded" (BA, 224). Val's decision to wander alone is like Orpheus's decision after he has looked back at Eurydice and lost her.[43] Although Val's choice of scene is not like that for Virgil's Orpheus who goes "far north through frozen fields and Scythian snows" (GEV, 119), the desert that Val chooses may be similar to the place chosen by Ovid's Orpheus, a place that "lacked any shade" (MET, 227).

In Virgil's and Ovid's texts, Eurydice is bitten by a snake, and so it is appropriate that *Battle of Angels* and *Orpheus Descending* be strewn with snake-references. In *Battle of Angels* Cassandra Whiteside compares herself to the Cassandra of antiquity who had "snake-bitten ears" (BA, 135). Valentine Xavier, nicknamed Snakeskin, wears a snakeskin jacket. Furthermore, as John Ditsky points out, Valentine Xavier is also associated with snakes because "the historical Valentine was an Italian doctor, a profession with the snake for its symbol."[44]

Perhaps because Val is so obviously a figure for Orpheus, many commentators have been quick to link Myra (renamed Lady in *Orpheus Descending*) to Eurydice. She is waiting for an Orpheus to lead her out of the hell/Hades in which she lives. Jabe, a stand in, if you like, for Pluto, ruler of the Underworld, calls the place, "artistic as hell" (OD, 109). Instead of being married to Val/Orpheus, Lady is married to Jabe, the owner of the dry goods store. Lady says, "I guess my heart knew that somebody must be coming to take me out of this hell" (OD, 135). Seeing that Mary is an obvious anagram for Myra, commentators have also associated her not only with the Virgin Mary, but also with Mary Magdalene.[45] In exploring the relation between Williams's texts and Virgil's and Ovid's pre-texts, however, I have noticed that there is also a kinship between Williams's Myra and Ovid's Myrrha, whose story is told in the same book of *Metamorphoses* as the Orpheus and Eurydice myth. There is a striking similarity between scenes involving a nurse figure. In both stories the nurse is horrified when she realizes that the lady is pregnant. In Ovid, this is because the lady (Myrrha) is carrying the child of an incestuous union with her father. In Williams, it is because the lady, Lady/Myra, is carrying the child of an adulterous affair with Val. More important, in both stories the ladies are turned into trees. In Ovid's account, this is Myrrha's punishment. She suddenly finds "roots thrusting from her toes" and "[her] blood became sap, her fingers twigs, her arms/ branches . . . her skin . . . hardened into bark" (MET, 240).

Lady/Myra uses tree imagery in *Battle of Angels* and *Orpheus Descending*. In the former she describes to Val how when she was a child, the family had a fig tree in the backyard that had never born fruit. Then suddenly one year it did bear fruit, and she decided to hang Christmas ornaments on it. "Oh darling," she says to Val, "haven't we any Christmas ornaments to hang on me?" (BA, 223). "Unpack the box!" she says in *Orpheus Descending*, "Unpack the box with Christmas ornaments in it, put them on me" (OD, 140). Lady again compares her body to a tree when she says, "This dead tree, my body, has burst in flower," and she shouts to her husband triumphantly, "I've won, I've won, Mr. Death, I'm going to bear!" (OD, 114). She has already aborted one child, and she will lose a second as she dies before the play is over.

With the ubiquitous tree imagery, an intertextual network is more firmly established between Williams's *Battle of Angels/Orpheus Descending* and Ovid's account of the Orpheus legend rather than Virgil's. Although Virgil says that Orpheus's music "made tigers tame and lured / The rugged oaks to follow" (GEV, 510), Ovid describes in much greater detail how Orpheus charms various trees to gather round him, to shade him. Ovid's list of trees includes the cone-shaped cypress tree that was once a boy, Cyparissus. In *Battle of Angels* cypress trees protect Val from the sunlight in Witches' Bayou: "Big cypress trees all covered with long grey moss the sun couldn't hardly shine through" (BA, 167). In a hut, Val makes love in a bed, "made out of cypress an' covered with heaps of moss" (BA, 170). Sandra, whose wrists Val "could snap . . . like twigs" (BA, 161), is always trying to lure Val to "Cypress Hill." This is the setting for the cemetery where she likes to make love listening to the one word that the dead have for the living, "Live!" (BA, 134; OD, 40).

The connection between Ovid's text and Williams's *Battle of Angels* and *Orpheus Descending* can be extended to other texts by Williams. The cemetery on Cypress Hill and the one word message from the dead is also to be found in the one-act play *The Case of the*

Crushed Petunias, where the word "live," we are told, "sounds much like the long, sweet sound of leaves in motion!" (AB, 30). These "leaves in motion" find their way into Tom Wingfield's closing soliloquy in *The Glass Menagerie*: "cities swept about him like dead leaves, leaves that were brightly colored but torn away from the branches" (GM, 115). In turn, these branches may remind us of "the broken stem . . . plummeting to earth" in Nono's poem in *The Night of the Iguana,* where the fruit on the orange branch cannot remain golden, and where again trees and people are associated when the speaker implores "Courage" to "Select a place to dwell / Not only in that golden tree / But in the frightened heart of me" (NI, 124). This "golden tree" can also take us back to the "golden tree" in *Orpheus Descending* that is part of the design on the curtain which screens off the bedroom/alcove. We see this tree clearly at the end of Act 2, Scene 4, when the curtain becomes "softly translucent with the bulb lighted behind it." After Lady goes through the curtain to join Val, "the stage darkens till only the curtain of the alcove is clearly visible" (OD, 102).

There are more trees in the epigraph to *27 Wagons Full of Cotton* taken from Sappho:

> Now Eros shakes my soul, a wind on the
> mountain falling on the oaks.

This short play involves the seduction of a young married woman, Flora, by the head of the Syndicate Plantation, whose name Silva is the Latin word for wood from which comes the Italian word *selva,* as in

> Nel mezzo del cammin di nostra vita
> mi ritrovai per una selva oscura,
> che la diritta via era smarrita.
>
> "In the middle of the journey of our life
> I came to myself in a dark wood where
> the straight way was lost."[46]

These are of course the first three lines to Dante's *Inferno,* which serve as the epigraph to *Camino Real.* From the word *selva* comes the word savage, which means literally, "of the woods, wild, uncivilized." We recall that Virgil tells us that with his music Orpheus successfully "lured / The rugged oaks to follow" (GEV, 119), and Ovid gives a great list of the trees that gathered around him (MET, 227), so the trees are associated in these pre-texts with seduction. In *Orpheus Descending*, seduction in an arboreal setting leads to lovemaking. We recall that Lady's father, "the Wop," planted an orchard on the north shore of Moon Lake:

> he covered the whole north shore of the lake with grapevines and fruit trees, and then he built little arbors, little white wooden arbors with tables and benches to drink in and carry on in, ha ha!
>
> (OD, 15)

Later, Lady and Val make love behind the curtain showing the "golden tree."

In *Suddenly Last Summer*, Catherine tells the Doctor that once when she was given a lift home from a party by a married man, he stopped the car near the Duelling Oaks at the end of Esplanade Street. "I think I got out of the car before he got out of the car," she says, "and we walked through the wet grass to the great misty oaks as if somebody was calling us for help there" (SLS, 65). "After that?" asks the Doctor, and Catherine explains, "I lost him.—He took me home and said an awful thing to me. 'We'd better forget it,' he said, 'my wife's expecting a child and —'" (SLS, 65). The trees for Catherine are aptly named, "the Duelling Oaks," for they provide the setting for an incident that causes her long-lasting pain and regret.

Although, as in the Witches' Bayou in *Battle of Angels*, trees may suggest a kind of idyllic Edenlike setting, the lovemaking over which they seem to preside often leads not only to pain and regret, but also, as in the case of Lady in *Orpheus Descending*, to death and destruction, with which they have already been associated through Carol's lovemaking in the cemetery on Cypress Hill. In *Suddenly Last Summer* this association between trees and death is made in the first stage directions, which describe Sebastian's bizarre garden in The Garden District:

> The colors of this jungle-garden are violent, especially since it is steaming with heat after rain. There are massive tree-flowers that suggest organs of a body, torn out still glistening with undried blood; there are harsh cries and sibilant hissings and thrashing sounds in the garden as if it were inhabited by beasts, serpents and birds, all of savage nature. (SLS, 9)

The violent colors and the suggestions of "organs of a body, torn out still glistening with undried blood" are reminders of Sebastian whose body was mutilated by native boys using knives and possibly the jagged edges of tin cans. Of course, Sebastian, a poet, is another Orpheus-figure, and like Val, he meets with an exceedingly violent death. In *Battle of Angels,* Val has his clothes torn off and is taken to the "lynching tree" (BA, 236). In *Orpheus Descending,* Val is killed by a blowtorch wielded by the savage Dawgs who are the equivalents to the Maenads.

Violence has been a preoccupation in Williams's texts since he first started writing. He wrote the short story, "The Vengeance of Nitocris" at the age of sixteen. Here, Nitocris, an Egyptian princess, avenges the death of her brother, the Pharaoh who is "torn to pieces" by the "clawing hands and weapons" of his own people (CS, 3). Following her brother's death, Nitocris secretly arranges the construction of a splendid amphitheater, and she invites the murderers of her father to a sumptuous banquet in the vault beneath it. With banquet tables, luxurious rugs, and "sparkling wines in abundance that would satiate the banqueters of Bacchus," she provides a "banquet scene difficult to resist" (CS, 7). Once the banquet has turned into a "delirious orgy," the empress leaves the revelers, and after ensuring that a stone blocks any hope they might have of leaving the cavern, she pulls a "wandlike" lever that opens sluice gates and causes torrents of water to gush into the cavern and drown all the revelers. For Nitocris, this is "a moment of supreme ecstasy"; she "lust[s] upon every triumph-filled second" (CS, 9). Eventually, she, herself, commits suicide, leaving only "her beautiful dead body" for "the hands of the mob" (CS, 12). In his foreword to *Sweet Bird of Youth,* Williams says of "The Vengeance Of Nitocris" that "it set the key note for most of the work that has followed" (SBY, xi). That key note is surely a kind of violence very similar to the Orphic violence described by Ovid and Virgil, for most versions of the Orphic legend begin with the violence entailed in the ravishment of Eurydice and end in the dismemberment of Orpheus.

Virgil tells us that the Thracian maids tore "Orpheus limb from limb / And hurled him piecemeal over the fields" (GEV, 119), but once again Ovid provides a more detailed pre-text for Williams's text. He describes how the women rush upon Orpheus with weapons that include "leaf-dressed lances" and "branches torn from trees." The women also acquire "heavy rakes / Hoes and long-handled mattocks," and they use them to destroy the cattle of fleeing farmhands. These gruesome implements provide them with even more effective tools for

Orpheus's dismemberment. Just as the trees participate in Orpheus's death, they participate in the vengeance that Bacchus, incensed by the loss of the "minstrel of his mysteries," wreaks on Orpheus's assailants. Bacchus attaches a root of a tree to each woman who, seeing "the bark creep up her shapely calves," attempted

> Distraught, to beat her thighs and what she struck
> Was oak, her breast was oak, her shoulders were oak
> Her arms likewise you'd think were changed to long
> Branches, and thinking so, you'd not be wrong. (MET, 251)

Although in Ovid's text, trees participate in this kind of destruction/transformation, they are also associated with mourning. Thus, following the death of Orpheus, the "forest trees cast down their leaves in grief" (MET, 250). In Williams's texts, trees are also associated with the mourning inherent in the gesture of looking back. In *Battle of Angels,* for example, Val looks back to the cypress trees and the bed of moss and cypress in the Witches Bayou. In *Orpheus Descending,* Lady looks back to her father's arboreal wine garden with so much nostalgia and regret that she attempts to recreate it in the confectionery store. At the end of *The Glass Menagerie,* Tom cannot help thinking of the life that he left behind as "the cities swept about [him] like dead leaves, leaves that were brightly colored but torn away from the branches" (GM, 115).

Trees, branches, leaves, and other arboreal references indicate one way in which Williams's texts may allude not only to one another, but also in particular to Ovid's *Metamorphoses,* and to a lesser extent Virgil's *Georgics* and even Dante's *Inferno.* The texts may be seen as looking back. Thus, *The Night of the Iguana* looks back to *Suddenly Last Summer,* which looks back to *Orpheus Descending,* which looks back to *Camino Real,* which looks back to *27 Wagons Full of Cotton,* which looks back to *The Glass Menagerie,* which looks back to *Battle of Angels,* which looks back to *The Case of the Crushed Petunias.* Although I begin the list here with *The Night of the Iguana* because it is the most recently written of the plays on the list, just as a later play may allude to an earlier play, an earlier one can allude to a later one.

On the whole though my tendency is like Roland Barthes' to "savor the ease which brings the anterior text out of the subsequent one."[47] Thus, when I come across the "Duelling Oaks" that haunt Catherine in *Suddenly Last Summer* I see an allusion to the "rugged oaks" that follow Orpheus in Virgil's account. When I read about Sebastian's death at the hands of the naked boys with their knives and jagged edges of tin cans in *Suddenly Last Summer* I think of the death of Orpheus at the hands of the Maenads armed with "leaf-dressed lances," "branches torn from trees," "rakes," and "mattocks" in Ovid's account. When I think of all those who look back with tear-filled regret in Williams's plays—for example, Myra/Lady (BA/OD), Tom (GM), Catherine (SLS), Nono (NI), Marguerite (CR), and of course Blanche DuBois (SND), I spot an allusion to Ovid's "forest trees" that "cast down their leaves in grief."

It also becomes difficult here not to think of the biographical subject, Tennessee Williams, as also caught up in the Orphic gesture of looking back. Here, I will argue that the melancholy looking back is reflected in Williams's work through the music of the blues, a counterpart to Orphic music.

Orphic Music and the Blues

When Orpheus descends to the Underworld he attempts to use the power of his music to move Pluto and Persephone to give him back his Eurydice. "To the music of his strings he sang," says Ovid, "And all the bloodless spirits wept to hear" (MET, 226). In most versions of the myth, after Orpheus loses his Eurydice for the second time, his melancholy music continues after his return to the upper world. Virgil compares his "sorrows" to those of the "the mournful nightingale" whose young have been stolen from her by man's "cruel hands" (GEV, 119).

Nightingales flutter through the titles of many of Williams's works. He entitled a very early play *Not About Nightingales,* and he later retitled *Summer and Smoke* (adapted from the short story, "The Yellow Bird") *The Eccentricities of a Nightingale.* In *Summer and Smoke,* Alma Winemiller, the daughter of a clergyman, has loved the boy next door, John Buchanan, since they were children. Much of the play concerns her loss of this, her one and only love. She reads Blake's "Love's Secret" to a group of ladies:

> I told my love, I told my love,
> I told him all my heart.
> Trembling, cold in ghastly fear
> Did my love depart.

(SS, 57)

She becomes another Orpheus-figure, an amateur pianist and singer referred to as "the Nightingale of the Delta." The Delta, of course, is the Mississippi Delta, and this was the home of many of the blues musicians of the 1930s including the notoriously brilliant Robert Johnson, whose song "Love in Vain" reminds me of Alma's poem:

And I followed her to the station: with a suitcase in my hand
Well it's hard to tell it's hard to tell: when all your love's in vain
When the train rolled up to the station: I looked her in the eye
Well I was lonesome I felt so lonesome: and I could not help but cry . . .[49]

Although I have been examining Williams's texts in terms of intertextual connection with the texts of Virgil and Ovid, the musical element allows Williams's texts to be read in relation to the blues—in terms of both its verbal and general suggestiveness, for as LeRoi Jones comments, "blues is primarily a verse form and secondarily a way of making music," and "there can be no such thing as poetry (or blues) independent of the matter it proposes to be about."[49]

Many blues lyrics deal with the subject of wandering of one kind or another. Here one might consider Blind Lemon Jefferson's "Easy Rider Blues," Black Ace's "Hitchhiking Woman," Gertrude "Ma" Rainey's "Yonder Comes the Blues," to mention only a few. Probably all blues singers, at one time or another, have sung about lonesome wanderers. In particular, the wanderer in "Yonder Comes the Blues," who spends his time walking beside a river, may remind us of the figure of Orpheus. At the beginning of Virgil's account, having already lost his Eurydice, Orpheus sings of her while "wandering lone upon a desolate shore" (GEV, 117). Ovid's Orpheus spends five days sitting on a river bank, "unkempt and fasting, anguish, grief, and tears / His nourishment," before wandering to a hill and finding some "open ground, all green with grass" (MET, 227). Williams's Val Xavier, another lonely wanderer, sings about his peregrinations:

My feet took a walk in heavenly grass.
All day while the sky shone clear as glass.
My feet took a walk in heavenly grass,
All night while the lonesome stars rolled past.
Then my feet come down to walk on earth,
And my mother cried when she give me birth.
Now my feet walk far and my feet walk fast,
But they still got an itch for heavenly grass.
But they still got an itch for heavenly grass.

(IWC, 101)[50]

The repeated phrase like line 1 repeated in line 3 and like line 8 repeated in line 9 was a hallmark of the blues. LeRoi Jones argues that the blues was derived from hollers and shouts, and "as was characteristic of the hollers and shouts, the single line could be repeated again and again, either because the singer especially liked it, or because he could not think of another line."[51] In Val's song, the singer's lonesomeness is compared to that of the stars. The song is a lament for the "heavenly grass," something that the singer has experienced but which he would love to experience again. His feet cannot take him back to the "heavenly grass" any more than Orpheus's feet can take him back to Eurydice. Notice, too, that, like Orpheus's song, Val's song is extremely seductive. It is only when "he begins to whisper the words of the song so tenderly that she [Lady] is able to draw the curtain open and enter the alcove" (OD, 102), and make love.

In *Orpheus Descending,* Lady asks Val to explain the writing on his guitar. He explains that these marks are the autographs of musicians: Leadbelly, King Oliver, Bessie Smith ["the name Bessie Smith is written in the stars"], and Fats Waller ["his name is written in the stars too"] (OD, 50–51). In *Orpheus Descending,* the blues takes the place of the Negro spiritual recordings that accompanied the action in the first production of *Battle of Angels.* We may recall that in *Battle of Angels* the Negro Loon hands his guitar to Val; Val then becomes the musician in *Orpheus Descending,* so that he is associated with the blues to the extent that even the moments leading up to his death are accompanied by the blues, for as the men search for him with their dogs, somewhere a "Dog Howl Blues" is being played (OD, 121).

Williams's first collection of one-act plays contains the blues in its title, *American Blues. Ten Blocks on the Camino Real* (precursor of the full-length play *Camino Real*) is the last play in the collection, and it is also the only play to feature the blues. In *Ten Blocks on the Camino Real,* a guitarist (who does not appear in the later version) is seated on stage as the curtain rises; he holds a blue instrument with which, as he stands, he "strikes a somber chord." His music is heard periodically throughout the play, especially in Block 4 where Marguerite recalls another guitar player, a young Gitano, who would not participate in the rituals that took place around a public fountain in a town in Provence. One night she threw a bouquet to the boy and later waited for him on his way home. "The stars," she says, "threw down their spears, and watered heaven with their ears" (AB, 54). Since the time of her "joy" with the Gitano, she has had many loves, but now she realizes that her youth has passed, and "I'm here," she says, "sitting with someone for whom I have no desire" (AB 54). Instead of Val's more generalized sense of loss—he grieves the loss of a place, the place of "heavenly grass"—Marguerite, like Orpheus, and like many of the blues musicians grieves the loss of one particular loved person. As Marguerite sits on a terrace expressing her grief the audience hears the "blue guitar," as it will do at the end of the play where "the music rises tenderly and richly as the Player of The Guitar steps into the moonlit plaza" (AB, 77).

Like Orphic music, then, the blues is associated with solitude and loss. Marguerite's feeling about the stars weeping may remind us of "the lonesome stars" in Val's poem. Her lack of desire for the person with whom she is sitting emphasizes her distance from people now, but the "blue guitar" may remind us of the intensity of her former passion. Although the "blue guitar" is played by a man, the music may be regarded as Marguerite's music. This is entirely in keeping with the blues phenomenon because, as LeRoi Jones points out, "the great classic blues singers were women."[52] In the Twenties, Howard W. Odum and Guy B. Johnson noted that among the extensive selec-tion of classic blues titles that they examined, "the majority of these formal blues are sung from the point of view of women . . . upward of seventy five per cent of the songs are written from the woman's point of view."[53]

W. S. Anderson argues that "whereas Virgil had made his central object the portrayal of irrational love as 'furor,' faulty though pathetic, Ovid inspects Orpheus's love and finds it wanting." In Anderson's opinion, Ovid indicates "the shallowness of Orpheus' feelings."[54] Ac-cording to Anderson, and I tend to agree, the real "furor" seems to belong more to Ovid's women: "Ovid's characters who are afflicted with passion, usually women," says Anderson, "are aware of its dan-gers, but struggle in vain to overcome it."[55] Thus, Myrrha's "furor" is much greater than that of Orpheus. Recalling Ovid's account of how "many a woman burned with passion for / The bard" (MET, 227), it is easy to see that Orphic music can reflect women's passion more than men's. Similarly, Williams's heroines are frequently more passionate than their male counterparts. In Battle of Angels and Or-pheus Descending, it is Myra/Lady and other women's passion for Val, rather than his passion for women, that is emphasized. In Ten Blocks, Marguerite's passion (at least, in her past) is emphasized more than Casanova's.

As in *Ten Blocks on the Camino Real,* a guitarist plays periodically throughout *The Purification.* With his music, he "weaves a pattern of rapture," which may focus our attention on both the sister's passion (with which "she went beyond all fences" [27W, 35]) and the Son's desolation following the loss of his sister. The Son believes that "truth is sometimes alluded to in music. / But words are too loosely woven to catch it in" (27W, 40), and so in the bare room where a trial is now taking place, he implores the guitarist to prompt him with music. As "the Guitar Player sweeps the strings" the Son contemplates, "How shall I describe / the effect that a song had on us? / Our genitals were too eager" (27W, 41). He describes their incestuous lovemaking with the kind of bird imagery so characteristic of Virgil and Ovid: theirs was a "coming of birds together," "a passionate little spasm of wings and throats" (27W, 45). Now, however, the Son desperately implores the musician to "weave back [his] sister's image," but it is too late:

> No. She's lost,
> Snared as she rose,
>   or torn to earth by the falcon!
>   No, she's lost,
>   Irretrievably lost.
>
> (27W, 41)

> Blue—
>   Blue—
>   Immortally blue
> is space at last . . .
> I think she always knew
> that she would be lost in it.
>
> . . . .
>
> For nothing contains you now,
> no, nothing contains you,
> lost little girl, my sister.
>
> (27W, 59)

There is clearly a parallel between the anguish that the Son feels following the loss of his sister and the anguish that Orpheus feels following the loss of Eurydice. Both seek solace in music. This longing for a sister/loved one to be restored may also be related to Tennessee Williams's own feelings following the loss of his sister, at least his sister's former self, lost to a lobotomy in the 1930s. Although the playwright's love for and devotion to his sister was undying a part of

Rose Williams, physical and mental, would always be "irretrievably lost."

Many of the possible Orphic parallels and connections with the blues that I have just explored in some of the early plays come together in *A Streetcar Named Desire*. Instead of the "blue guitar" of earlier plays, music is provided, in particular, by a "blue piano." Never one to mince words, Elia Kazan says that "the blue piano catches the soul of Blanche," and he argues that "the blues is an expression of the loneliness and rejection, the exclusion and isolation of the Negro and their opposite longing for love and connection. Blanche too is 'looking for a home,' abandoned, friendless. 'I don't know where I'm going, but I'm going.'"[56] We should not, however, see the blues as exclusively belonging to Blanche, any more than the blues is exclusively the Sister's in *The Purification*. In that play, the blues also reflected the feelings of the brother. In *A Streetcar Named Desire*, the blues is linked at different times to many of the characters. In scene 3, for example, after Stanley's outburst during the poker game, the black musicians around the corner play a song called "Paper Doll." They play it "slow and blue." Stanley has lost Stella, his "baby doll." As he tries to call upstairs, "the 'blue piano' plays for a brief interval." Eventually, slowly, and with the sound of "low clarinet moans" in the background, Stella comes down the staircase, and Stanley "falls to his knees on the steps and presses his face to her belly, curving a little with maternity" (SND, 60). The scene may recall to some, the Son's comment about the musician in *The Purification*:

> His song, which is truth
> is not to be captured ever.
> It is an image, a dream,
> It is the link to the mother . . .
>
> (27W, 40)

The blues music here in *A Streetcar Named Desire* may be depicting the inevitability of separation of mother and baby—with Stanley as the crying baby losing his mother, Stella, whose belly is "curving a little with maternity." At other moments in the play, the blues may be played for Stella. The "blue piano" music in scene 7 can be associated with Stella's feelings about losing the Blanche she once knew. At the end of the play, holding her baby wrapped in a pale blue blanket, Stella cries out her sister's name three times, "Blanche! Blanche! Blanche!" (SND, 142). This reminds me of the moment in

Virgil's text when the name, Eurydice, is heard three times as Orpheus's dismembered head floats down the Hebrus to the sea:

> Its death-cold tongue cried forth "Eurydice!"
> The parting breath sighed "Poor Eurydice!"
> "Eurydice!" the sounding shores replied.
>
> (GEV, 119–20)[57]

Stella goes out on to the porch and "sobs with inhuman abandon." "There is something luxurious," we are told, "in her complete surrender to crying now that her sister is gone" (SND, 142). Although the Son in *The Purification* has to live with the death of his sister, Stella too loses a sister—this time not to death, but to the madhouse.[56] In spite of these possibilities, however, Kazan is right to suggest that the blues is essentially Blanche's music. The "blue piano" is playing throughout scene 1, but the music grows louder when Blanche describes the loss of Belle Reve. The music may represent Blanche's loneliness and exclusion from the conjugal scene in scenes 2, 4, and 5 because in scene 2, Stanley announces Stella's pregnancy; in scene 4 Stanley and Stella embrace as Stanley grins through the curtains at Blanche; and in scene 5 Steve and Eunice chase each other, and Stella and Stanley go off arm in arm. Her exclusion from the family scene is also marked in scene 9 where Mitch tells her that she "is not even clean enough to bring in the house with [his] mother" (SND, 121). The "blue piano" may also point to her loneliness in scene 8 when Mitch fails to show up for Blanche's birthday supper, and in scene 10 when Shep Huntleigh fails to materialize.

The "blue piano" may also be seen as providing background music to remind us of the great loss that Blanche, like Orpheus, has had to endure: the loss of a young love. The "blue piano" is heard at the crucial moment in the newsboy scene when the boy is looking for a way out. "Young man! Young man, young man!," says Blanche, "Has anyone ever told you that you look like a young Prince out of the Arabian Nights?" (SND, 84). The repetitions of the word "young" may remind us of her young love Allan Grey, "The Grey Boy" (SND, 96).

As *A Streetcar Named Desire* draws to a close, then, when we hear "the swelling music of the 'blue piano' and the muted trumpet" (SND, 142), we should think of the blues as primarily Blanche's music. Although the action of the play takes place in "Elysian Fields," Blanche has not found paradise, the "heavenly grass" of which Val sang. Like

Val, like Orpheus, the archetypal poet of the West, Blanche has no home; and like the characters in Samuel Beckett's *Waiting for Godot* or Williams's own late play, *The Two-Character Play*, she has no place to which she can escape: she has quite simply nowhere to go.

Williams announces in his introduction to *A Streetcar Named Desire*, "On a Streetcar Named Success," that "the monosyllable of the clock is Loss, Loss, Loss, unless you devote your heart to its opposition," and loss is indeed a central concern of both Orpheus and Blanche. Orpheus loses his Eurydice (in fact, he loses her twice—at the beginning of the story she is already lost and then with the fateful look back he loses her again). Blanche loses her Allan Grey. These losses cause Orpheus and Blanche incalculable sadness, and to express this sadness words alone are inadequate, and hence the need for music.

In *Conversation with the Blues*, Paul Oliver transcribes several interviews that he has had with blues musicians, and tries to establish a definition of the blues. Lil Son Jackson comments

> Well I think the blues is more or less a feeling that you get from something that you think is wrong, or something that somebody did wrong to you. . . . That's the way I see the blues. It cause a sad feeling, more or less a sad feeling about it, and when you have that sad feeling well, quite naturally you reproduce it.[59]

Of course, Blanche thinks that she has done something wrong. She feels guilty about telling Allan that he disgusted her—for this provoked his suicide, and Blanche is haunted by this, not only through the blues but also through the polka music and the sound of the gunshot. Surely, Orpheus feels that he has been wronged by those who have taken away his Eurydice, and perhaps he feels too that he must share in the responsibility for the loss that followed his fateful look back.

Also in *Conversation with the Blues*, Edwin Buster Pickens maintains that

> The only way anyone can ever play blues—he's got to have them. . . . No man in good spirit, no man in good heart can sing the blues, neither play them. . . . But nach'al blues come directly from a person's heart. . . . You have a tough way in life—that makes you blue. That's when you start to sing the blues, when you've got the blues.[60]

In his "Historical and Critical Text" that accompanies W. C. Handy's

A Treasury of the Blues, Abbe Niles suggests that as far as the blues is concerned,

> the essential element is the singer's own personality. Whatever is said is in some way brought back to him; he deals in his own troubles, desires, resentments, his opinions of life and people. There seems even to be room left for his pleasures. Happy blues are rare, but some have an invincible optimism . . . Melancholy, however, is most frequently the theme; there is no doubt that the name "blues" was bestowed on the tunes because of the mood of the verses.[61]

In *A Streetcar Named Desire,* Blanche is the character melancholy enough to sing the blues. She is the character who suffers most the pangs of lost love. She is the character, like Orpheus, who has no home. She is the character who has the most experience of solitude. Perhaps the song that she sings in the bathtub could be sung to a blues accompaniment. Like many blues ballads, "It's Only a Paper Moon" combines the lament for lost love with the feeling that without that love the world is phony:

> Without your love,
> It's a honkey-tonk parade!
> Without your love,
> It's a melody played
> In a penny arcade
>
> .   .   .   .
> It's only a paper moon,
> Just as phony as it can be—
> But it wouldn't be make-believe
> If you believed in me!
>
> .   .   .   .
> It's a Barnum and Bailey World,
> Just as phony as it
> can be—

(SND, 100–101)

As Stanley and Stella hear her singing and the sound of running water, they can also hear "little breathless cries and peals of laughter . . . as if a child were frolicking in the tub" (SND, 101). They might wonder whether Blanche's gaiety is feigned, "phony," like the world depicted in the song, or is this one of those rare happy blues? Undoubtedly, Blanche has "got the blues." With her song, "It's Only a Paper Moon," perhaps we can hear some of that "invincible optimism" that Abbe

Niles talked about. Perhaps Blanche attempts to cover up her profound and ineluctable sadness, but according to LeRoi Jones, "the blues, as it came into its own strict form, was the most plaintive and melan-choly music imaginable."[62] Not only does the blues clearly retain this plaintive and melancholy aspect today, but these were also the charac-teristics of Orphic music. Orpheus may have been the first musician, but the blues may be as old as his music. Blues artist Boogie Woogie Red explains

> I'll tell you about the blues—the blues is something that you play when you're in a low mood or something. . . . And the average person takes the blues as just a plaything, but the blues is really serious. The blues is something that you have to play coming from your heart. And blues have been goin' on for centuries and centuries, and the blues was written years and centuries ago—they was always here.[63]

I am suggesting, then, that there is a place for the playwright in the intertextual network that brings together the blues and the Orphic. The adjectives that spring to mind here are plaintive, melancholy, and relentless. The intertextual resonances that I have established here may provide us with more accurate pointers to the author's biographi-cal self than traditional source studies would. A part of the intertex-tual network, however, still needs to be examined, and that is the part to which we now turn our attention: the suggestiveness of the proper name.

Exploring the Proper Name

The titles of all texts invoke the concept of naming because as titles they automatically name the texts to which they refer. In the case of *A Streetcar Named Desire*, not only does the title name the play written by Tennessee Williams, but naming also takes place within the title itself. The word *streetcar* is being used to name desire. As the play begins, the question of naming prefigured by the title is taken up by the characters. Blanche, for example, gets confused when she says to Eunice, "I'm looking for my sister, Stella Dubois." As she remembers that Stella's name has changed, she corrects herself, "I mean—Mrs. Stanley Kowalski" (SND, 15). When Stella arrives, Blanche calls her affectionately: "Stella, oh, Stella, Stella for Star!" (18). Here, Blanche interprets Stella's name, finds the star in it, and answers the unvoiced question, "What does the name Stella stand for?" with "Stella, oh, Stella, Stella for Star!" Blanche will use the addendum "Stella for Star" frequently when talking to or about her sister.[64]

"Stella for Star" is the first of a number of astronomical/astrological references in a play that was once entitled *Blanche's Chair in the Moon,* a play where a newsboy sells papers for "The Evening Star" (Blanche jokes "I didn't know stars took up collections" [82]), and where Blanche looks in the sky for "the Pleiades, the Seven Sisters" (86). With Stanley, Blanche will discuss astrological signs, indicating that her birthday is on the fifteenth of September and that she is therefore "a Virgo." "What's Virgo?" asks Stanley. Blanche explains "Virgo is the Virgin" (77). Here Blanche, inadvertently perhaps, is also making sense of her name. In a sense, she is speaking out of her name, for to be a virgin is to be untouched, pure, clean, as in *virgin snow.* This is not to say that Blanche is a virgin, but through her name, she is linked to whiteness and to virginity. During the Poker Night scene, Blanche glosses her own name when meeting Mitch for the first time:

> *Mitch.* Deal me out, I'm talking to Miss—
> *Blanche.* DuBois.
> *Mitch.* Miss DuBois?
> *Blanche.* It's a French name. It means woods and Blanche means white, so the two together mean white woods. Like an orchard in spring! You can remember it by that.
>
> (54–55)

Of course, Blanche's commentary here is inaccurate because "white woods" in French would be *bois blanc.* If the adjective and noun are to be taken together as Blanche suggests, they should agree with each other in terms of gender; in other words, the adjective *blanche* would have to be *blanc* to agree with the noun *bois,* which is masculine.[65] Thus, the name Blanche DuBois presents us with a confusion of gender.

In English the verb "to blanch" can mean "1. to take the color out of and make white: BLEACH . . . . 2. to make ashen or pale. . . . 3. to give a favorable appearance to: WHITEWASH, GLOSS—often used with over" (*Webster's*). Of course, I am making use here of homophones, that is words that sound alike even though their meanings may be different. When we hear the name, Blanche, then we may hear the verb "blanch," and we can think of Blanche blanching—trying to make her world white, pure, innocent, virginal; trying to gloss, to gloss over.[66]

Blanche is blanching, for both in her name and in her language, she is constantly glossing, in the sense of giving explanations or interpreta- tions (for example, "Stella, Stella for Star" or "white woods" for Blanche DuBois). To gloss can also mean "to veil or hide [something that would otherwise be objected to or prove a source of difficulty] by some plausible pretext, subterfuge, pretense or excuse" (Webster's). Despite her claim, "I've nothing to hide" (40), Blanche always seems to be hiding something. In fact, she is hiding the confusion of gender and sexual orientation in her name. Although Blanche is obviously female, she can also be seen as male.

George Michelle Sarotte points out that although novels containing homosexuals were acceptable when A Streetcar Named Desire first appeared in 1947 it was not acceptable to have homosexual characters appear on or even off-stage.[67] It was more acceptable for homosexual characters to appear in fiction. Williams then, focuses more directly on the homosexual in his short stories—for example, "The Mysteries of the Joy Rio" (1941), "The Angel in the Alcove" (1943), "The Resemblance between a Violin Case and a Coffin" (written in 1949), "Hard Candy" (begun in 1949, finished in 1953), and "One Arm" (begun in 1942, finished in 1945). Stanley Hyman, however, has sug- gested that Williams employs "the Albertine Strategy," that is to say, disguises homosexual males as females as Proust had done in changing the name Albert to Albertine in A la recherche du temps perdu."[68]

Notice that Stanley Kowalski offers us the possibility of reading Blanche as gay male when he says, "What queen do you think you are?" (emphasis added; 127) Even the first audiences of A Streetcar Named Desire may have been aware of the homosexual connotations of the term "queen." "Homosexual" is one meaning of "queen" given by the New Dictionary of American Slang: "A male homosexual, espe- cially one who ostentatiously takes a female role." According to this dictionary, the homosexual sense of "queen" appeared as early as the late nineteenth century. There is evidence that in 1949, Tennessee Williams himself was using the term "queen" in the homosexual sense. In a letter to Maria St. Just dated 9 October 1949, Williams writes: "Well, the town is blooming with British queens, mostly connected in some way with the ballet."[69]

Similarly, Mitch's observation, "I was fool enough to believe you was *straight*" (emphasis added; 117) can make us think of Blanche as not straight, as homosexual. The *Dictionary of American Slang* defines the adjective "straight" as "1. Undiluted, neat; said of liquor. 2. Honest; normal. Depending on the context, denotes that the person referred to is not dishonest, not a drug addict, not a homosexual, and so forth." The *Dictionary* further specifies that the uses "sexually normal and/or not a drug-addict" have been employed since 1945. Thus, we may infer that like "queen" the sexual connotations of "straight" may have been familiar to the first audiences of *A Streetcar Named Desire*. Although we may feel that Mitch means that he thought that Blanche was honest, we can still hear "straight" as heterosexual. In her numerous sexual experiences with boys, Blanche may be regarded as both heterosexual woman often described by critics as "nymphomaniac" and as gay male. The name Blanche DuBois, then, opens up confusions of gender and sexuality that it is difficult to deny.

In English "blanch" can also mean "to bleach by excluding light" *(Webster's)*. Rarely leaving the apartment in the daytime, Blanche is a creature of the night. "Her delicate beauty must avoid a strong light" (15). She claims that she cannot endure the sight of "a naked light bulb" (55). Living in darkness, she becomes increasingly pale (blanch), as white perhaps as the clothes that she wore when she first arrived: white suit, gloves, and hat (15), but one has the feeling that the whiteness of her clothes and her name hide something, something dark. She is attracted to innocence, just as a moth is attracted to the light. We know, however, that Blanche is no virgin. She has freely given herself, her whiteness (including her virginity) to the boys; but for the most part, she conceals this fact, hides it beneath her white apparel and beneath her name.

Her name may also be appropriate for her marriage may never have been consummated and would therefore be *une marriage blanche*. This is clearer in the movie version of the play. Gene Phillips points out that for Kazan's movie version, Williams had to rewrite Blanche's speech about Allan Grey in order to tone down the homosexuality— in other words, to avoid the reference to Blanche finding her young husband in bed with another man.[70] Instead, in the movie, then, Blanche describes how on their wedding night she pretended to sleep but heard Allan crying. With the implication that Allan is impotent in the marital bed, the possibility of his being gay is not erased and the possibility of *une marriage blanche* is more striking than in the play.

Of course, there is a part of Blanche that wants to appear "virginal," "white," *blanche*, a "lily."[71] But the other side of Blanche wants to speak, refuses to hold back, refuses to remain silent, insists that she is no virgin. In French, *blanche* means white, but it is also the musical term in French for a half note. Furthermore, isn't *blanche* a combina- tion of *bl* and the French *anche* which means "reed," a rustic musical pipe. Moreover, Blanche tells Mitch that in French *bois* "means woods and Blanche means white, so the two together mean white woods. Like an orchard in spring!" (SND, 55). This wood in Blanche's name pulls together all the references, not just to woods but orchards and trees and branches and leaves and twigs that we have seen scattered throughout Williams's texts and pre-texts.

Notice also that Blanche imagines the area outside the Kowalski apartment to be "the ghoul-haunted woodland of Weir!" (SND, 20). Given her name, how appropriate that Blanche DuBois, Blanche of the Wood, should imagine a wood even in the heart of New Orleans. The reference, of course, is to Edgar Allen Poe's "Ulalume—A Bal- lad," another possible pre-text in which a poet grieves the death of a loved one. Describing this poem in *The Encyclopedia Britannica,* Theodore Watts-Danton suggests that "the poet's object . . . was to express dull and hopeless gloom in the same way that the mere musi- cian would have expressed it—that is to say, by monotonous reitera- tions, by hollow and dreadful reverberations of gloomy sounds. . . . 'Ulalume' properly intoned would produce something like the same effect upon a listener knowing no word of English that it produces upon us."[72] Both musically and thematically, the leaves which are "crisped and sere," may be like those at the end of *The Glass Menag- erie,* and the cypress trees like those in *Battle of Angels.* Poe's poem fits neatly into the intertextual network established here. Curiously, in French, *bois* can also refer to the woodwind instruments or section of the orchestra. Thus through the *blanche* (half note), *anche* (reed) and *bois* (wood + woodwind instrument), Blanche DuBois seems inex- tricably tied both to woods (trees), music, and Orpheus.

In "The Garrulous Grotesques of Tennessee Williams," Ruby Cohn points out that "anglicized Blanche's name is Duboys, and under her chaste surface, Blanche lusts for boys."[73] Blanche frequently refers to her husband as a boy. At the end of scene 1, Blanche tells Stanley, "The boy—the boy died" (SND, 31). In the next scene she protects Allan's letter, "Poems a dead boy wrote," from the touch of Stanley's hands (42). Even Stella forces us to see that Allan was only a boy:

"she [Blanche] married a boy who wrote poetry" (102). After the death of "the Grey Boy" (96), Blanche used to entertain the young soldiers returning to barracks after a night on the town (120). Later, after "many intimacies with strangers," she lost her job at the school because of an involvement with a seventeen-year-old boy (118). She is clearly attracted to the newsboy in scene 5 and to Stanley who refers to himself as a boy in scene 10. ("Not once did you pull any wool over this *boy*'s eyes!" [emphasis added; 127]). And then in the last scene of the play, she muses wistfully about a young doctor who she dreams will be by her bedside the night she dies (136). It seems very appropriate then to read Blanche DuBois as Blanche DuBoys— Blanche of or from the boys.[74]

This reading of Blanche DuBois as Blanche DuBoys also provides further ground for seeing in Blanche an allusion to Orpheus. In Virgil's *Georgic* IV, Orpheus's rejection of or indifference toward the women who are attracted to him can be seen, as suggested by Emmett Robbins, as "simply the result of the singer's undying attachment to the woman he has lost."[75] W. K. C. Guthrie points out, however, that following the loss of Eurydice, and his subsequent shunning of the company of women, "he [Orpheus] did not avoid the report which so often attaches to those who lead celibate lives, of having another outlet for his passions."[76] For some commentators, Orpheus therefore became "the originator of homosexual love."[77] Ovid leaves us in little doubt concerning Orpheus's sexual relations with boys, for we are told that while "Orpheus held himself / Aloof from love of women . . . / It was his lead that taught the folk of Thrace / The love for tender boys" (MET, 227).[78] Therefore, through her actions as a lover of boys, and through her name, Blanche DuBois, Blanche DuBoys, Blanche may again be seen as alluding to Orpheus.

If we look back for a moment to the trees that gather around Orpheus, we may observe that two of the last to join the group are a pine tree, formerly the young Attis, and a cypress, formerly the young Cyparissus, both boys loved by gods. W. S. Anderson concludes that in Ovid's account, Orpheus' song "features pretty young boys, not Eurydice."[79] Orpheus, who teaches "the love for tender boys" is, like Blanche, the seducer of boys. Now it seems that Blanche is closer both through her name and actions to Orpheus, than Val is to Orpheus. In *Battle of Angels* and *Orpheus Descending,* Val shows no signs of attraction to young boys. In fact, the emphasis in the play is on how others are attracted to him. Notice that he is also frequently described as a boy. In *Battle of Angels,* Myra reads Val's letter of recommenda-tion from an old employer in which the employer says, "This here boy's peculiar" (BA, 147). Lady tells Val early in *Orpheus Descending,* "Boys like you don't work" (OD, 48). Near the end of that play, Talbott warns Val: "Boy, don't let the sun rise on you in this county" (OD 121). Were Val to be transplanted from *Orpheus Descending* to *A Streetcar Named Desire,* there is no doubt that Blanche would desire him. She may be like Virgil's Orpheus, constantly mourning the loss of her young love (in her case a boy), but like Ovid's Orpheus, she is also the lover of boys and in this role may be regarded as a stand in for Tennessee Williams.

Orpheus, Blanche DuBois, and Tennessee Williams

Williams has repeatedly claimed, "I am Blanche DuBois"[80] and has identified with her, particularly in terms of a shared hysteria (CN, 228). Also like Blanche, Williams had a tendency to lie. One example of this is Williams's and Blanche's shared propensity to mislead people concerning their age. Of course, Blanche pretends to be younger than her sister. Donald Windham describes how Williams deceived people at the time he was 29 by pretending to be 25. The trick was exposed when at the opening night of *The Glass Menagerie,* his mother looked into the program and said, "Why son, this write up has your age wrong."[81] The affinity between Williams and Blanche was also appar-ent to several observers. Truman Capote, for example, who was in the audience for the opening night of *A Streetcar Named Desire* in 1947, describes how "the stars, Jessica Tandy and Marlon Brando took sixteen curtain calls before the 'Author! Author!' demands were met. He was reluctant to be led on stage, this young Mr. Williams. He blushed as though it were the first time that he had ever been kissed by strangers. . . ." Capote concludes his tribute with these reflections, sparked by the sight of the young playwright on stage:

> Tennessee was an unhappy man, even when he was smiling the most, laughing the loudest. And the truth was, at least to me, that Blanche and her creator were interchangeable; they shared the same sensitivity, the same insecurity, the same wistful lust. And suddenly, as one was thinking that and was watching his bows to the deafening clamor, he seemed to recede on the stage, to fade through the curtains—led by the same doctor who had guided Blanche DuBois toward undesirable shadows.[82]

Although Capote had known Tennessee Williams for a long time and had spent enough time with him to make the aforementioned observations, Capote was by no means the first to sense a Blanche/Williams parallel. In fact, Elia Kazan, who directed the first stage productions of A *Streetcar Named Desire* as well as the movie, wrote

> Blanche DuBois, the woman, is Williams. Blanche comes into a house where someone is going to murder her. The interesting part of it is that Blanche DuBois–Williams is attracted to the person who's going to murder her. . . . I saw Blanche as Williams, an ambivalent figure who is attracted to the harshness and vulgarity around him at the same time that he fears it because it threatens his life.[83]

The two texts that I have quoted here, one by Capote, the other by Kazan, are two examples of biographical interpretation. The logic is simple. I know that Williams is like this—Blanche is like this—therefore Blanche and Williams are interchangeable. I do not believe that Capote's reading of Blanche as Williams or Kazan's reading of Blanche as Williams are wrong. One could say that both Capote and Kazan knew Williams—Capote claims to have known Williams since he (Capote) was sixteen years old[84]—both assume they know the "real" Williams. Surely they knew different Williamses, not just because they were with him at different times, but because both would have formed different impressions of Williams; both would have represented him to themselves in different ways.

Blanche wants to keep sexuality in the dark, to avoid switching on the lights—a naked light bulb might reveal truths about her sexual history like her predilection for boys and the fact that she has enjoyed so much sexual freedom. This is comparable to Williams's own sexual history, and at this stage in his career he does not want his sexual history to become public knowledge. At the time that Williams was writing A *Streetcar Named Desire*, homosexuals were marginalized to such an extent that even Williams did not want his homosexuality to become public knowledge although it had been common knowledge in the theater for some time. He made it public knowledge in an interview with David Frost in 1970 (CN, 146). In 1971, Williams complained, "Now high school kids, delinquents I imagine, race past my house in Key West in their cars at night shouting, 'Queer! Faggot!'" (CN 189). Ten years later he claimed "it's . . . still dangerous to be openly homosexual" (CN 344).

People frequently see the homosexual as needing help. Thus Blanche makes it sound as if she was the person (counsellor? doctor? priest?) to whom the young homosexual, Allan Grey, came for assistance: "He wasn't the least bit effeminate looking—still—that *thing* was there. . . . He came to me for help" (emphasis added; SND, 95). Soon after the marriage began, however, Blanche realized that she "wasn't able to give him the help he needed but couldn't speak of!" Thus, in her confession in scene 6, Blanche moves from talking about the "thing" that Allan himself could not speak about (his homosexuality) to "the terrible *thing* at the edge of the lake" (emphasis added), Allan's dead body.

I emphasize the word *thing* because Williams's use of the word is absolutely in keeping with its use in the ancient Greek world. In his monumental *History of Sexuality*, Michel Foucault points out that the Greeks apparently referred to the act of having sex with a boy as "doing the thing." Foucault discusses a Greek "reluctance to evoke directly and in so many words the role of the boy in sexual intercourse: sometimes quite general expressions are employed such as 'to do the thing' [*diaprattesthai to pragma*]; other times the 'thing' is designated by the very impossibility of naming it."[85] Foucault also emphasizes that in the Greek world "in the sphere of sexual ethics, it was the juvenile body . . . that was regularly suggested as the 'right object' of pleasure. And it would be a mistake to think that its traits were valued because of what they shared with feminine beauty."[86] The juvenile body found in Williams's texts fits in well with this Greek model. In *A Streetcar Named Desire,* Blanche is careful to point out that Allan "wasn't the least bit effeminate looking" (SND, 95).

The Greek model is also relevant to Williams's short stories. In "The Resemblance between a Violin Case and a Coffin" the narrator argues that there was nothing wrong with "adoring the beauty of Richard. It was surely made for that purpose, and the boys of my age made by such ideals of beauty and grace" (CS, 277). He then refers to the legend of Pico della Mirandola and the woman who fainted as she saw him enter the city of Florence on a "milkwhite horse in a storm of sunlight and flowers." "'He will pass in the time of lilies,' she exclaimed." The idea here, a very Greek one, is that we must catch the beauty of the young male body somehow before it grows old. In "One Arm" Oliver Winemiller is eventually sent to the electric chair, and then his body is sent to a medical college. This body, which has been the focus of the male gaze throughout the story, intrigues even "the men performing the dissection" who "were somewhat abashed by the body under their knives. It seemed intended for some more august purpose, to stand in a gallery of antique sculpture, touched only by light through stillness and contemplation, for it had the nobility of some broken Apollo that nobody was likely to carve so purely again" (CS, 188). The male body as object of desire in Williams's texts is characterized then according to the Greek ideals of grace without effeminacy.

Curiously, Williams also uses the word *thing* to describe his *Memoirs,* a work that can also be regarded as a confession. Williams employs the word *thing* in the first sentence: "To begin this 'thing' on a socially impressive note (MS, 1). Although he says later, "Now obviously this 'thing' has dealt so far mostly with the vicissitudes of my lean and green years as a writer" (MS, 83), for many readers the thing was the detailing of his adventures as a homosexual. The enormous crowds that gathered at the Doubleday Fifth Avenue bookstore in the fall of 1975 waiting for the playwright to autograph copies of the book and the subsequent appearance of the book on the bestseller list may have a lot to do with what Dakin Williams and Shepherd Mead describe as "hints of unspeakable secrets now revealed."[87]

Clearly Blanche blames herself to some extent for Allan's suicide. On the dance floor at Moon Lake Casino, Blanche had said bitterly to Allan, "I saw! I know! You disgust me" (SND, 96), and this is quickly followed by the suicide. After seeing "the terrible thing at the edge of the lake," Blanche, like Orpheus, is trapped in a perpetual cycle of speaking (which for Orpheus takes the form of singing) and looking back. At Moon Lake she looked back to the scene of Allan's homosexual act and uttered the word "disgust." Now in telling Mitch the story, she looks back again. She was unable to stop herself speaking then (uttering the word "disgust"); she is unable to stop herself now— stop herself from speaking, from speaking about sexuality.

Foucault argues that we can never complete the task of putting our sex, "a universal secret, an omnipresent cause, a fear that never ends,"[88] into words. This is precisely the task in which Blanche and Williams are engaged—it is the reason why she cannot stop speaking, and perhaps to some extent why Williams cannot stop writing. Since the beginning of the play, she has hardly stopped speaking. The first scene provides a good indication of her loquaciousness. This is particularly striking because Blanche draws attention to Stella's relative silence: "Precious lamb! You haven't said a word to me" (19). Apparently it has always been like this because Stella replies, "You never did give me a chance to say much Blanche. So I just got into the habit of being quiet around you" (20). When Blanche raves about the demise of Belle Reve she again draws attention to Stella's silence: "And now you sit there telling me with your eyes that I let the place go" (27). Blanche will frequently say something and then feel the need to clarify it: "I didn't mean to be rude, but—" (18), "What am I saying I didn't mean to say that. I meant to be nice about it" (19), and when Stella eventually leaves the room in tears, Blanche says, "Forgive me I didn't mean to—" (27). The torrent of words in scene 1 lead to Blanche's closing words in scene 1 which are about Allan Grey: "The boy—the boy died," and the violent emotions triggered by this memory makes Blanche exclaim, "I'm afraid I'm—going to be sick!" (31). Only the necessity of bodily functions can stop the flow of her words.

Later Blanche confesses to Mitch that since Allan's death, she has been sexually involved with a series of strangers: "intimacies with strangers seemed all I seemed to be able to fill my empty heart with" (118). Blanche has done everything she could to conceal her sexual history but has decided that there is no point in concealing it any longer. She is also nudged into confession by Mitch's forcing her into the light:

> Mitch. You never want to go out till after six and then it's always some place that's not lighted much.
> Blanche. There is some obscure meaning in this but I fail to catch it.
> Mitch. What it means is I've never had a real good look at you, Blanche. Let's turn the light on here.
> Blanche [fearfully]. Light? Which light? What for?
>
> (116)

The hapless Mitch eventually does switch the light on, and as he stares at Blanche, "she cries out and covers her face" (117). Mitch is attempting to see through the makeup, the false whiteness, and to bring the truth of her sexuality into the light.[89] Earlier Mitch told Blanche, "I like you to be exactly the way you are, because in all my experience I have never known anyone like you" (87); but now it is clear that he does not know exactly how she is and has never really known who she is.

Blanche can either leave sexuality in the dark, the darkness that she claims to prefer, the darkness that she hides, conceals, blanches, glosses over, veils with paper lanterns, so that we cannot see it; or, through confession, bring sexuality into the light. Finding her husband engaged in a homosexual act, Blanche sees her husband as trans-gressing a boundary, violating an unwritten law, which is not only the boundary between marital fidelity and infidelity, but also the boundary between heterosexuality and homosexuality. In a sense Blanche has condemned the Grey boy for transgressing boundaries, but then she herself as lover of boys becomes the transgressor of bound-aries. Perhaps she is like the Grey boy—both are outsiders, living on the border, living on the edge. Furthermore, they are both Orpheus figures—Allan is a homosexual poet. Blanche describes his love letters as poems "yellowing with antiquity" (41), as "poems a dead boy wrote" (42). Thus, although it is mainly through Blanche that Wil-liams transforms his sexuality and his sexual past into discourse, he may also be doing this through Allan Grey, the young homosexual.

As well as modeling Blanche on himself, to some extent Williams models his own life on Blanche. Thus, Williams weaves many of Blanche's statements into his life. He echoes Blanche when he says, "I have never blamed anyone for anything but deliberate cruelty, for there has always been in me the conviction of Blanche, that 'deliberate cruelty is the one unforgivable thing'" (MS, 170). Blanche's exact words are "Some things are not forgivable. Deliberate cruelty is not forgivable. It is the one unforgivable thing in my opinion and it is the one thing of which I have never, never been guilty" (SND, 126). Thus, "I shall never cease to be sensual—even on my deathbed," says Williams. "If the doctor is young and handsome, I shall draw him into my arms" (CN, 232). Here, he reflects Blanche's longing, for she too wanted to die, "with her hand in the hand of some nice-looking ship's doctor, a very young one" (SND, 136). Like Blanche, Williams also expresses a desire to be buried at sea. Blanche says,

> And I'll be buried at sea sewn up in a clean white sack and dropped overboard—at noon—in the blaze of summer and into an ocean as blue as . . . my first lover's eyes. (SND, 136)

There is a reverberation here of the death of Hart Crane. In turn, Williams echoes his character in this codicil to his will, which he wrote while staying at the Hotel Élysée in 1972. It is reproduced for us by Dotson Rader:

> I, Thomas Lanier (Tennessee) Williams, being in sound mind upon this subject, and having declared this wish repeatedly to my close friends—do

hereby state my desire to be buried at sea. More specifically, I wish to be buried at sea at as close a possible point as the American poet Hart Crane died by choice in the sea; this would be ascrnatible [sic], this geographic point, by the various books (biographical) upon his life and death. I wish to be sewn up in a canvas sack and dropped overboard, as stated above, as close as possible to where Hart Crane was given by himself to the great mother of life which is the sea: the Caribbean, specifically, if that fits the geography of his death. Otherwise—whereever fits it [sic]. (TCH, 345)

Here again Williams appears to weave some of *A Streetcar Named Desire,* specifically, a character's desire to be buried at sea, into his own life, or more specifically, into his own imagined death and burial. Notice that Blanche's words provide a more elliptical allusion to Hart Crane's death than Williams's words in the codicil. She does not even mention Hart Crane—she merely mentions the sea and being dropped overboard and the "clean white sack" that becomes the "canvas sack" in the codicil. Notice also that Williams has confidence in the biographer's ability to convey factual information, the facts concerning the precise location of Crane's suicide.[90] In "'Minting their Separate Wills': Tennessee Williams and Hart Crane," Gilbert Debusscher points out that on a slipcover for his own recording of some of Crane's poems, Williams shows his awareness of the facts of Crane's life. Williams culled the information in part from a biography of Crane written by Philip Horton and a collection of letters edited by Brom Weber. According to Debusscher, Williams was particularly interested in "the most intense moments of Crane's life, the day of his suicide and the emotionally charged night immediately preceding it. Of the latter we are told that Crane "had visited the sailors' quarters and the visit had turned out badly. They had treated him mockingly and violently."[91] In Williams's texts, Debusscher finds numerous echoes from Hart Crane and presents compelling evidence to suggest that the hold that Crane had over Williams was "biographical as well as poetic." Debusscher lists a large number of traits including Crane's "bohemian wanderlust that prevented him from settling down permanently" and Crane's "sexuality" which together with other traits constitute "a personality in which Williams must have recognized himself as in a mirror."[92]

In terms of the intertextual network that I have established, then, Crane can now join the company of Orpheus, Blanche, and Williams, particularly on the basis of attraction to boys and as a perpetual wanderer. We should note that just like Orpheus, Hart Crane can only exist for Williams as part of a text. Thus, Williams cannot base the plans for his burial on the burial of Hart Crane, but on the way that Hart Crane's death has been represented in written texts—especially biographies. Furthermore, when Williams says that he is Blanche, he is really saying that the image that he has of himself, or the way that he, if you like, textualizes himself, corresponds to Blanche. He represents himself to himself, and then says that he is Blanche. Similarly, for Capote and Kazan and all who try to see Tennessee Williams as Blanche, this Williams can only be the Williams as they represent him to themselves.

In addition to the other meanings of "bois" in French already mentioned *bois* is the first and second person singular form of the verb, *boire,* to drink. In the first scene when Blanche is left alone for a second in the Kowalski apartment, she "springs up," rushes to a closet and helps herself to a drink (SND, 18). When Stella arrives, Blanche pretends not to know where the liquor is: "Open your pretty mouth and talk," she says to Stella, "while I look around for some liquor." Seizing the liquor from the closet, Blanche is shaking so much that Stella offers to pour the drinks and suggests a coke to go with the whisky. "Just water, baby, to chase it!" says Blanche (19). Later, after an evening out with Mitch, she again searches desperately for liquor: "This crashing around in the dark is my search for some liquor" (87), and the phrase she uses when she finds some—"Just enough for two shots without any dividends, honey" (88)—reveals that she is probably an experienced drinker. She cannot get enough to drink. We cannot believe that one is her limit (21) or that she rarely touches it (30) or that she has never seen Southern Comfort before: "Southern Comfort! What is that, I wonder?" Blanche DuBois, as Mitch so eloquently puts it, "has been lapping it up all summer like a wild cat!" (115).

Like Blanche, Tennessee Williams was hopelessly addicted to alcohol. While in Rome in the early fifties, he wrote a letter to the director, Cheryl Crawford, saying that "he could not walk a Roman street unless there was a bar or a wineshop."[93] In 1969, after being hospitalized and given "the cold turkey treatment" for his chronic addiction to pills and alcohol, Williams speculated about "how adversely [his] work was affected by the pills and liquor, which had both become an uncontrollable urge" (CN 148). "I was living a life in the Sixties," he says, "deep under the influence of pills and liquor around the clock" (CN 185). It is easy to see a correspondence between Blanche DuBois,

Blanche of Drink, and the Williams that is portrayed in these statements taken from letters and interviews.

As we saw, Williams further acts out another part of Blanche's
name, Blanche DuBoys, Blanche of or from the boys. The two components of the name, drink and boys, come together in this passage from
Tennessee: Cry of the Heart:

> Bars were about his [Tennessee's] favorite places on earth, and in every
> city he had particular watering holes that he frequented. In London, for
> example, he loved the bar at the Savoy, and Joe Allen's, Annabel's, and
> Tramps. And he used to taxi up to Hampstead Heath to drink at King
> William's Pub, where the boys were. In Chicago it was the Pump Room,
> and in New York the Monkey Bar, Joe Allen's, the bar at the Sherry-
> Netherland and the Four Seasons. And for boys, the Haymarket, Cowboys
> and Cowgirls, and later Rounds, a saloon off Third Avenue that attracted
> an uptown clientele—well-dressed young men, often models, who were
> up for grabs and for sale. (TCH, 149)

For the Williams of this description, the obsessive need for alcohol
and the obsessive need for boys are inseparable.[94] The "watering hole"
contains or leads to the boy. Similarly, Blanche DuBoys is inseparable
from Blanche of Drink. The two occur together again in a particularly
striking fashion in the Newsboy scene:

> *Blanche.* You—uh—didn't get wet in the rain?
> *Young Man.* No, ma'am. I stepped inside.
> *Blanche.* In a drug-store and had a soda?
> *Young Man.* Uh-huh.
> *Blanche.* Chocolate?
> *Young Man.* No, ma'am. Cherry.
> *Blanche [laughing].* Cherry!
> *Young Man.* A cherry soda.
> *Blanche.* You make my mouth water. [*She touches his cheek lightly, and
>   smiles. Then she goes to the trunk.*]
> *Young Man.* Well, I'd better be going—
> *Blanche [stopping him].* Young man!
>
> (SND 83–84)

In her attempted seduction of the young man, unsure perhaps what
to say, Blanche turns to the subject that is constantly on her mind:
drink. Admittedly, she is asking about soft drinks here, but earlier in
the same scene she has been laughing at Stella for offering her a coke—
"Why, you precious thing, you! Is it just coke? . . . a shot never does
a coke any harm!" (79).

She is obsessed with drink. One may think that it is not the thought of the drink, a "cherry soda," that supposedly makes her mouth water—it is the young man: "You [as a young man] make my mouth water." The other meaning, however, "You [because you mention a drink] make my mouth water," is also possible. This sentence provides a smooth transition from the drink (Blanche as Blanche of Drink) to the young man (Blanche as Blanche DuBoys). The boy looks for an exit—he "clears his throat and looks yearningly at the door"—but Blanche is looking "yearningly" at him. "Come here," she says softly, "I want to kiss you, just once, softly and sweetly on your mouth!" (84). This orally fixated Blanche has moved from talking about her mouth watering to expressing her desire to kiss the boy's mouth. Her thirst for a drink and her thirst for the boy are one: the one kiss recalls the one drink ("One's my limit" [21]). Then, "without waiting for him to accept, she crosses quickly to him and presses her lips to his" (84). After the kiss, she says "Now run along, now, quickly! It would be nice to keep you, but I've got to be good—and keep my hands off children" (84). She could also try keeping her hands off liquor, but as Blanche DuBoys and Blanche of Drink, she cannot keep her hands off either.

In *Memoirs,* which came out in 1972, Williams portrays himself as sexually incontinent as Blanche. He too cannot keep his hands off boys. He gives particularly vivid descriptions of how he acted on his own predilection for boys—for example, after going out to California during the war, he frequently used to pick up young servicemen who hung out in the Palisades of Santa Monica:

> I would strike a match for a cigarette. If the matchlight confirmed my first impressions of his charms, I would mention that I had a pad only a few blocks away, and he would often accept the invitation. If the first one or two were not to my satisfaction, I would go out for a third. (MS 78)

The way that Williams represents himself here goes much further than our earlier examples to link the representation to Blanche not just in terms of sensuality, or attraction to boys, but in terms of a need for a large number of sexual partners. Who knows how many boys from the army camp, later picked up in the paddy wagon, which came to "gather them up like daisies" (SND, 120), were having sex with Blanche? Who knows how many of the men (or boys) in Laurel were having sex with her? Stanley and Mitch clearly suspect large numbers, and again one may be tempted to see Blanche as Williams's textualiz-ing of himself.

Williams gives even more lurid accounts of the activities of Wil-liams, the lover of boys, in his letters to his then friend, Donald Wind-ham. In this passage, he describes the result of another encounter at the Palisades:

> I have just had an orgy with a Ganymede of 15 years exactly, met on the Palisades. Moaned like a wounded bird pierced twice by the arrow of love, and I have just sent him home to get there ahead of Mama who works on the swingshift.[95]

In Greek mythology, Ganymede, said to be the most beautiful youth in the world, became cupbearer to Zeus after Zeus had "disguised himself in eagles' feathers and abducted him from the Trojan plain."[96] In the letter, then, if the boy, Ganymede, "moans like a wounded bird," the "I" too becomes associated with birds. We recall that in Ovid, Orpheus was surrounded by a flock of birds, (MET, 229) and that in Virgil Orpheus' grief was identified with that of the grieving nightingale. Gore Vidal says he used to call Williams the Glorious Bird: "I had long since forgotten why until I reread the stories. The image of the bird is everywhere."[97] As an example, I would suggest this description of lovemaking by the Son in *The Purification:*

> Resistless it was,
> this coming of birds together
> in heaven's center . . .
> Plumage—song—the dizzy spirals of flight
>
> .   .   .   .
> a passionate little spasm of wings and throats
> that clutched—and uttered darkness.
>
> (27W, 45)

In *Orpheus Descending,* Val is compared to a bird, a special kind of bird; he is like one of the birds he describes, birds that

> live their whole lives on the wing, and they sleep on the wind . . . like other birds fold their wings and go to sleep on a tree . . .—never light on this earth but one time and they die! (OD, 56)

The striking image of the bird is again used to describe Williams in this passage by Dotson Rader:

yet his curiosity, his sexual or affective needs were such that he ventured where it wasn't safe to be. I don't simply mean the young men we met or the various dives and bars he accompanied me to. I mean his compulsion to travel, to stay in flight like some land bird lost over the vast sea. (TCH, 180)

In these texts, then, there is a coming together of Val, Orpheus, and Williams. Furthermore, the bird in continual motion, staying in flight, never lighting on the earth, is like Williams's texts in that they are not tied to a convenient origin (the Father, author), but are caught up in an interextual network, as we have seen, involving trees, music, birds, and figures like Orpheus, Blanche DuBois, Hart Crane, and Williams—traces of other texts seemingly without end. The writing, however, goes on. No one has the last word. Williams writes in "Orpheus Descending," an early poem,

> and it will not be completed
> no, it will not be completed
> for you must learn, even you, what we have learned,
> that some things are marked by their nature to be not
> > completed
> but only longed for and sought for a while and abandoned.
>
> (IWC, 28)

The incompleteness of the writing does not signify the end of writing or that the writing has stopped. On the contrary the writing goes on. The corpus and the intertextual network become more and more extensive. As long as he lived, Williams, whose typewriter, like Val's guitar or Orpheus' magic lyre, was his "life's companion" (OD, 57), never seemed to lose his desire to write.

Living in New Orleans in 1938 and early 1939, waiting tables and distributing handbills for a jazz club, Williams was so poor that, as he later told an interviewer, he "had to hock everything but [his] typewriter to get by."[98] For Tennessee Williams, life without a typewriter—life without writing—was, and always would be, inconceivable, as inconceivable as a life without boys. "There are only two times in this world when I am happy and selfless and pure," wrote the young Williams to Donald Windham. "One is when I jack off on paper and the other when I empty all the fretfulness of desire on a young male body."[99] In an interview he confessed, "There is no pleasure in the world like writing well and going fast. It's like nothing else.

It's like a love-affair. It goes on and on and doesn't end in marriage. It's all courtship" (CN, 11).

In Ovid's account of the death of Orpheus we are told that after he had been slain, Orpheus' head and lyre floated down the river:

> Hebrus' stream received his head
> And lyre, and floating by (so wonderful!)
> His lyre sent sounds of sorrow and his tongue,
> Lifeless, still murmured sorrow, and the banks
> Gave sorrowing reply.
>
> (MET, 250)

Perhaps Orpheus' continuing to sing and his instrument's perpetual emission of "sounds of sorrow," even and in spite of Orpheus' death, can be compared to Williams's continual writing, and Williams's song, which, with the continuing productions of his plays years after his death, can still be heard.

In 1935, according to Spoto, Williams felt a powerful association with the poet Rainer Maria Rilke. At that time Williams was at Washington University, and "that year the *Sonnets to Orpheus* were snatched up by campus poets and professors everywhere" (KS, 49). In this chapter, we may at times have seemed to part company with this figure from whom all music emanates and to whom all music returns, but, in fact, throughout this work on intertextuality we may have never really left him.

> His metamorphosis
> is in this, and this. No other name
> should trouble us. Once and for all,
> when there's song, it's Orpheus. He comes and goes.[100]

Despite Williams's choking to death, his music, like Orphic music, is still heard. In fact, couldn't we say that now, "once and forever / it is Williams where there is song?" or "once and forever / it is Blanche where there is song?" Just as we have seen the suggestion that there is no origin to the blues, it could be argued that there is no origin to song. Williams's own signature tune may be like the music that he specifies in *The Glass Menagerie* as "the lightest and most delicate music in the world and perhaps the saddest" (GM, 9).

Although Williams's death is still shrouded in some mystery, Williams is dead. Donald Spoto explains

> On the evening of February 24, 1983, he withdrew quietly to his bedroom with a bottle of wine. On his bedside table was the traditional array of prescriptions—capsules, tablets, eyedrops, and nosedrops and all the paraphernalia associated with decades of hypochondria and chemical dependence. It was later reported by the New York medical examiner and the pathologist that during the night Tennessee Williams had ingested small quantities of a variety of drugs—cocaine among them—with the wine, and that a barbiturate overcap had somehow lodged in his throat: apparently he had used that cup like a spoon, to swallow two Seconal capsules. He had been, it seemed, unable or unwilling to summon help. (KS, 365)

Rader's account is slightly different. He tells us, for example, that Jon Uker, a paid companion, was sleeping in an adjacent room and also that Williams, at that time was seventy-two years old, and "was in bad health, fatigued, and often disoriented, melancholy, nearly blind, and ineffably lonely. He suffered from a loneliness like a growing wound, unstanchable, a wound he no longer could heal nor tried to disguise" (TCH, 338–39). Apparently dismissing Spoto's idea that Williams may have been "unwilling to summon help," Rader, without giving the source of his information, tells us that Williams tried to call for help.

> He took two seconals just before he went to sleep.
> Sometime before morning he woke, and half-asleep in the darkness he searched to find another Seconal to help him back to sleep. By mistake he picked up the plastic bottle cap [this was from an eyedrop bottle] and put it in his mouth. It stuck in his throat and choking he gagged loudly. Trying to summon help, he toppled out of bed, knocking over the nightstand. It made a crash that Jon heard in the other room. He ignored it.
> Tennessee choked to death. (TCH, 339)

By mentioning the wine and detailing the various kinds of pills, Spoto portrays a Williams who may remind us of Blanche as Blanche of Drink and Orpheus—in his connection to Bacchus, to whom Williams once referred as the "inebriate god" (WL, 57). By mentioning Jon in the room next door, Rader, on the other hand, may be portraying a Williams who reminds us of Blanche as Blanche DuBoys and Orpheus who "taught the folk of Thrace / The love for tender boys" (MET, 227). Rader's description of Williams's feeling a loneliness like "a growing wound" may also remind us of Orpheus' loneliness. Furthermore, Rader's Williams does not give up on life: he was "trying to summon help," and in this effort to carry on, Williams is like Blanche

who, in spite of terrible grief and talking about dying eating an un-
washed grape and so on, never even hints at suicide; and he is like
Orpheus who pleads "with hands outstretched" with the Thracian
women who are about to slay him. (MET, 250) Perhaps Williams's
hands too were outstretched as he tried to call for help.

Williams, Blanche, and Orpheus, then, are caught up in an intertextual network. We cannot make simple equations between Orpheus
and Williams or Blanche and Williams because each separate individual is difficult to define. I have suggested that Blanche may be defined
as Blanche DuBoys or Blanche of Drink, and with his predilections
for boys and drink Williams may be like Blanche here; but of course,
in defining Blanche in these terms I restrict Blanche, I exclude other
possible ways of defining her, ways which may preclude any identifi-
cation of Williams with Blanche. Thus, in spite of Williams's claim
that he is Blanche DuBois and despite all the similarities between
author and character, Williams is and is not Blanche, just as he is and
he is not Orpheus. Furthermore, Williams is and is not "The Glorious
Bird" (the nickname given him by Gore Vidal) flitting through his
texts. Like the bird that Val says never touches the earth, Tennessee
Williams, the author, is never able to attain an absolute presence in
his texts, a presence that is outside of the intertext.

In one interview Williams uses the tree image to express the idea of
union as opposed to separation. He is talking about his grandparents:

Baucis and Philemon, yes, that's what they were like. . . . I thank God
that I have seen exemplified in my grandmother and grandfather the possibility of two people being so lovingly close as they were that they were
almost like a tree. Two people that had grown into a single tree. (CN, 87)

An account of the myth is to be found in Ovid. Baucis and Philemon,
a couple who have grown old together, are rewarded for their kindness
toward the disguised gods, Jupiter and Mercury, by having their wish
to die at the same time granted. After dying, they are not transformed
into one tree, as Williams recalls, but two trees growing side by side.[101]
Allusion would appear to be everywhere: Blanche alludes to Williams; trees in Williams's texts allude to trees in Ovid's texts; Val's
guitar alludes to Orpheus' lyre, and so on. Perhaps Val, who plays a
guitar covered in blues musician's signatures, and Blanche, who loves
boys and alcohol, and sings in the bathroom allude to Orpheus, "the
ministrel of [Bacchus's] mysteries" (MET, 251). But it may be equally
true to say that allusion is nowhere: in its playfulness, as Derrida has

suggested, allusion is never certain. Because of the inevitable play in allusion, the figure in the text and the figure alluded to cannot be as one: so the trees/people in the myth can only be "almost *like* one tree" (emphasis added), but never one tree.

Tennessee Williams dies because a bottle cap lodged in his throat and he suffocated. Windham implies that Williams himself would have been very amused to read about a playwright dying in this way, particularly one who had predicted for forty years that he would die of heart trouble. He would have greeted the description with "a wild whoop of laughter" like the one Windham had heard many years ago when Williams read in a newspaper that "an old man in a wheelchair had been set fire to and burnt to death when he fell asleep with his lit cigar in his mouth."[102] Windham explains Williams's outlook like this, "Tennessee looked at life then with the distant view of comedy, rather than with the near view of tragedy, because his personal trage-dies were so close to the center of his emotions that to preserve his saneness, he had to look at them as if they were far off."[103]

Williams's laughter may detract from the Orphic parallel. It is hard to imagine Orpheus laughing. Williams's music may like Orphic music and the music of the blues musicians be melancholy, but Williams's laughter is almost legendary.[104] On the other hand, one should be careful, I think, not to be taken in by Williams's laughter. It could just be a pose, a distancing device as Windham suggests. Capote may also have been right when he suggested that "Tennessee was an un-happy man, even when he was smiling the most, laughing the loudest."[105]

Postmodern literary biography is very much aware that any attempt to render the biographical subject is inevitably linked to the generally unstated interests of the person making the biographical claim. Thus Rader's Williams is a function of Rader's affection for Williams, the man. Spoto's portrayal is much less tinged with romanticism or senti-mentality. Capote's and Windham's Williamses are somewhere in be-tween.

As for the intertextual approach, we may have found Williams in the tree, in Blanche, in Val, on a guitar, in the blues, in the birds, or in Orpheus. Intertextuality teaches us that, in Roland Barthes's terms, writing "traces a field without origin—or which, at least has no other origin than language itself, language which ceaselessly calls into ques-tion all origins" (IMT, 146). If Williams is present in his texts, then, it is not as origin, as author—God, as guarantor of meaning, but as simply one thread in a vast intertextual fabric. His life (the *bios* in biography) is a fiction or play that makes a great contribution to this fabric, producing at times exquisite patterns. Perhaps the most extraordinary pattern in Williams's corpus and life is the one that surrounds and incorporates the name Blanche DuBois.

3

The Effects of Signature

The subject of writing does not exist if we mean by that some sovereign solitude of the author. The subject of writing is a system of relations

—Jacques Derrida

Like Barthes' textual analysis, Derrida's deconstructive project is not concerned with recapturing or reproducing any particular meaning that an author intends his or her language to convey. For Derrida there is an excess in writing that takes texts beyond an author's signifying intention. In *Of Grammatology,* Derrida argues that "the writer writes *in* a language and *in* a logic whose proper system, laws, and life his discourse by definition cannot dominate absolutely" (Derrida's emphasis; OG, 158). Texts then escape the shackles of authorial intention. At the same time, rather than being in control of their language, authors are used by that language. Instead of attempting to guess what was on the writer's mind, readers are faced with a different task. Thus, Derrida continues, "the reading must always aim at a certain relationship, unperceived by the writer, between what he commands and what he does not command of the patterns of the language that he uses. This relationship is not a certain quantitative distribution of shadow and light, of weakness or of force, but a signifying structure that critical reading should *produce*" (Derrida's emphasis; OG, 158).

This "signifying structure" is not reducible to the supposed "content" of a text. Derrida is extremely wary of "the security with which the commentary considers the self-identity of the text, the confidence with which it carves out its contour, [and which] goes hand in hand with the tranquil assurance that leaps over the text toward its presumed content, in the direction of the pure signified" (OG, 159). Although recognizing the useful function of thematic criticism, Der-

rida has reservations about thematic criticism's insistence on the leap
to theme, for in making this leap critics inevitably subjugate signifiers
to the semantic.

Rather than being concerned with thematicism, Derrida seems
much more interested in the nature of the attachment between signifiers and author. Again, I should emphasize that it is simply not true
to say that deconstruction does not concern itself with the author.
Indeed if deconstruction, as some would have us believe, denies any
attachment between signifiers and author, then why has Derrida
dwelt so persistently on the question of signature? In "Signature,
Event, Context," Derrida draws on the work of Austin who distinguishes between oral and written utterances. Austin points out that
with an oral statement in the first person, the person doing the uttering is referred to simply by virtue of "*his being the person who does
the uttering.*" "Written utterances (or 'inscriptions,')" however, are
linked to the source, "by his [the author's] appending his signature
(this has to be done because, of course, written utterances are not
tethered to their origin in the way spoken ones are)."[1] Like Barthes,
Derrida questions this tethering of text to origin, but rather than
substituting intertextual connection for filiation as Barthes has done,
Derrida looks more closely at the possibility or impossibility of filiation, in an attempt to specify the nature of signature.

In this early essay Derrida expresses himself quite unequivocally
when he answers his own question, "Are there signatures?" by saying,
"Yes, of course, everyday. The effects of signature are the most ordinary thing in the world" (MR, 328). We may think here of the way
that we sign checks everyday. Our signatures authenticate the checks.
Signatures provide the link between our checks and ourselves. They
allow us to cash in on our signatures. "In order to function," says
Derrida, "that is, in order to be legible, a signature must have a repeat-
able, iterable, imitable form; it must be able to detach itself from the
present and singular intention of its production" (MR, 328).

Although a person's signatures may appear to be all the same, indeed
they need to appear to be all the same in order to function, no two
signatures will be exactly alike. The signature then depends on both
repetition and difference, and this seems to be what is meant by itera-
bility. Furthermore, for Derrida the principle governing signatures is
the same as the principle governing texts in general in that they have
the ability to function independently of the intentions of the signee
(who in the case of texts is the author). The signature effect is pro-

duced by the signature itself just as the effect of a text is produced by the text itself independently of authors' intentions. This does not mean, however, that the connection between signature (text) and signee (author) is lost or that signature effects should be ignored by those involved in the biographical project.

As an example, here, one might take the case of Jacques Derrida himself. As Jane Marie Todd points out, "In colloquia and interviews, Derrida is asked to answer criticism of his texts; seminars, university courses, articles and books are dedicated to the work of Derrida. All of this assumes that the proper name 'Derrida' means something; that the signature designates Derrida as responsible; and that his texts have a natural relation to him."[2] Derrida chooses to close his "Signature, Event, Context," which is also the last essay of *Margins of Philosophy*, with his own signature accompanied by the parenthetical note: "*Remark*: the—written—text of this—oral—communication was to have been addressed to the *Association of French Speaking Societies of Philosophy* before the meeting. Such a missive therefore had to be signed. Which I did, and counterfeit here. Where? There. J. D." (MR, 330). One point here is that the written text may always appear to be signed but the signature can never quite be the same and may therefore be regarded as counterfeit. Also Derrida's playful "Where? There" points to the difficulty of locating the signature, a preoccupation of much of his later work.

In *Glas* (1974), Derrida explores the signatures of Hegel and Genet, and monumentalizes them in separate columns. In Genet, he finds *genet*, a type of horse native to Spain and also *genêt*, a type of flower, and he sees Genet's writings as capitalizing on these associations. In Hegel, Derrida notes the wing *(aile)* and the eagle *(aigle)*, which function as motifs in Hegel's writing. At the same time, Derrida again returns to his own signature because for Genet and Hegel to sign their texts, according to Derrida, he, the reader, the scriptor of the new text, *Glas*, must also sign. Each signature, in other words, requires a countersignature. Thus in the right column Derrida introduces his own initials in a discussion of Genet's *Pompes Funebres*, substituting "J. D." for "J. G.", making use of the happy coincidence that his initials are those of the dead man, Jean Decarnin, whose funeral has a vital role in Genet's text. Furthermore, Derrida inverts his initials to form D. J., "déjà": "I am accessible, legible, visible," he says, "only in a rear view mirror."[3] "When I sign, I am already dead [I am D. J. dead]. I hardly have the time to sign than I am already dead, that I am already dead. I have to abridge the writing, hence the siglum, because the structure of the 'signature' event carries my death in that event" (19bi).[4] The cause of death may not be obvious. Is Derrida simply returning to Barthes' death of the author or does the author die in the act of signing because to sign is to place oneself outside of one's text? In *Glas*, Derrida plays on the French word *tombe*, which can function as both noun and verb. "The *seeing* falls to the [tomb]stone" (2b). The signature erects itself as both a monument or tomb, and the signature falls: hence what Gregory L. Ulmer calls "the monumentality and mourning inherent in the separation of the speaker from the word in writing."[5]

Derrida includes the biographical when he lists some possibilities for interrogating a text "from apparently extrinsic instances" (GL, 3b). Readers of a text make assumptions about a text's "outside." Biographical readers, for example, make assumptions about the author. The implication is that no matter what assumptions we make about a text's outside, we should take account of the signature as the articulation between the inside and the outside. If it is inside, the signature "no longer signs, operates as an effect within the object, plays as a piece in what it claims to appropriate or to lead back to its origin. The filiation is lost" (4b), or as Derrida puts it in *Signéponge/Signsponge* (1976), "by not letting the signature fall outside the text . . . and by inserting it into the body of the text you monumentalize, institute, and erect into a thing or stony object. But in doing so, you also lose the identity, the title of ownership over the text: you let it become a moment or part of the text, as a thing or common noun" (S/S, 56). In this case, then, the signature cannot function as the source of the text or point toward an origin, father, author. If, on the other hand, the signature is outside the text, "the signature emancipates as well the product that dispenses with the signature, with the name of the father or of the mother the product no longer needs to function. The filiation again gives itself up, is always betrayed by what remarks it" (GL, 4b).

Notice that in *Glas* Derrida indicates that the author may be thought of as mother rather than or as well as father. More important, with the signature as outside, a text may be thought of as complete without it, as functioning independently of the author, and as, in a sense, then, having killed off its father/mother. There is obviously a conflict between text and signature. J. M. Todd explains,

The text tries to liberate itself from the signature, to engage in a play of signification without being encumbered by the signature, which, in turn, works to reduce the play of signification by returning the text to its source, reducing the effects of language by centering the meaning of the text in the author's intentions. Signature and text work against each other, each trying to consume or bury the other.[6]

Nevertheless, because of its position on the border between inside and outside, the signature does establish the link between author and text. This phenomenon cannot be without importance for the biographical project.

If (s)he is inside the text, then, the author cannot be outside it as its owner, controlling the text. So, the "place" of the signature, argues Peggy Kamuf,

is not a place at all, but an always indivisible limit within the difference between writer and work, "life" and "letters." Signature articulates the one with the other, the one *in* the other: it both divides and joins. It is the double-jointedness of signatures that will be lost to any discourse that continues to posit a continual exteriority of subjects to the texts they sign.[7]

Rather than thinking about straight forward filiation, literary biography needs to be concerned with this border.[8] As Randolph Gashé puts it, "The biographical is thus that internal border of work and life, a border on which texts are engendered. The status of the text—if it has one—is such that it derives from neither the one nor the other, from neither the inside nor the outside" (ED, 41).

In *Signéponge/Signsponge,* Derrida continues to explore signature effects, this time focusing on the figure of Francis Ponge. Here Derrida argues that there are three modalities of the signature. The first modality, the "nominal signature" which is "the signature in the proper sense [which] represents the proper name, articulated in a language and readable as such: the act of someone not content to write his proper name (as if he were filling out an identity card), but engaged in authenticating (if possible) the fact that it is indeed he who writes" (S/S, 52–54). I am not concerned with Tennessee Williams's "nominal signature"—the signature that he used to satisfy autograph hunters, the signature a reproduction of which we see after removing the dust jacket, duplicated, engraved on the front cover of the hardback edition of his *Collected Stories,* the signature that indicates legal ownership, which indicates that a certain text or body of texts are the property of Tennessee Williams.

Derrida describes the second modality as "the set of idiomatic marks that a signer might leave by accident or intention in his product." He argues that "we sometimes call this the style, the inimitable idiom of a writer, sculptor, painter, or orator" (S/S, 54). In considering this modality, we do not need to consider the writer's intention to sign in a particular way. Although reading for a signature does not involve reading for authorial intentions, Derrida is not, however, denying that writers/signatories have intentions.

Of the third modality, which Derrida admits is "more complicated," he says, "we may designate as general signature, or signature of the signature, the fold of the placement in abyss where, after the manner of the signature in the current sense, the work of writing designates, describes, and inscribes itself as act (action and archive), signs itself before the end by affording us the opportunity to read: I refer to myself, this is writing, I am writing, this is writing—which excludes *nothing* since, when the placement in abyss succeeds, and is thereby decomposed and produces an event, it is the other, the thing as other, that signs' (Derrida's emphasis; S/S, 54).

In this chapter I consider the second and third modalities of the signature. For the second I again turn to A *Streetcar Named Desire*. This time instead of seeing Blanche DuBois as part of an intertextual network I see her as caught in a signifying structure that places her in opposition to Stanley Kowalski. As a signature event, though, an opposition in terms of specific characters is clearly inadequate, and it is necessary to attempt to somehow shift attention away from the vagaries of the thematic and back to style. The "set of idiomatic marks," then, that constitute the signature, in its third modality, are to be found, then, on the surface of Williams's text. The approach here is in keeping with postmodernism's predilection for surface rather than depth.

If the components of Tennessee Williams's signature that I find in A *Streetcar Named Desire* are really components of his signature, then, these same components must be found in other texts by Tennessee Williams; so later in this chapter I attempt to find the same signature that I discovered in A *Streetcar Named Desire* in Williams's *Suddenly Last Summer*. In fact, this "stylistic signature" must be found not only in these two plays, but also throughout the Williams corpus.

In the second part of this chapter I turn to the more complicated third modality of the signature. Williams himself has shown his awareness of the limitations of intentionality when he suggests that as far as a play is concerned, "many of its instants of revelation are wayward flashes, not part of the plan of an author but struck accidentally off" (WL, 57). In other words, activity is taking place within his language of which he is not originally and indeed may never be aware. A corollary of this idea is that Williams may not sign, leave his mark, in any way that he intends. With the third modality of the signature, it is the work of writing itself that takes over, especially the notion of writing as consisting of a number of levels but no center.

Of course, we are back now to the question of play, but instead of turning to the play of the name as I did in the previous chapter, I now turn to the play between inside and outside, between what may be seen as the writing's center and that which surrounds the center. There is a connection here between this *mise en abyme* structure and the biographer's nostalgia for an innocent center, which any deconstructive reading is likely to bring into question. To say that there is no center, however, is not to deny the existence of a subject.

*   *   *

Beyond Thematicism: Williams's Stylistic Signature

A good example of a thematic approach to Tennessee Williams is Alfred Adler's *A Streetcar Named Desire: The Moth and the Lantern.* Adler suggests a whole system of dichotomies represented by the two main characters in *A Streetcar Named Desire*, Stanley and Blanche. He sees Stanley as predator, victimizer/executioner with Blanche as moth/victim. He also puts Desire (Eros) in Stanley's world, opposing it to Death (Thanatos) in Blanche's. It is easy to question these dichotomies. I have already shown, for example, that Blanche may be thought of as predator—she preys on young men. Furthermore, and not unrelated to this, why are we to assume that the desire named in the title or the desire that names the streetcar is Stanley's desire, men's desire? What about Blanche's desire? What about women's desire?

At the end of scene 10, Blanche strikes ineffectually at Stanley with a broken bottle top; catching her wrist, Stanley calls the woman "Tiger!—tiger!" (SND, 13) This scene has been hotly disputed by audiences, throughout the world. Whereas, some people, like Adler see Blanche as the victim of rape, others see her as attempting to satisfy her desire. In fact, Williams himself has suggested that Blanche was a tiger and that "she surrendered to him out of desire" (CN, 110). It seems to me, however, that there is always a problem when the male order (which includes Williams as reader of his own text) as-sumes that it understands female desire.

In scene 2, just after Blanche's arrival in Elysian Fields, Stanley wants to delve into the trunk to find out more about her, her past, and especially the loss of Belle Reve. In doing this, we can see him as trying to understand, to lay bare the space of the feminine. Having already pulled some of the clothes out of the trunk earlier in scene 2 when Blanche was in the bathroom, Stanley continues to ransack the trunk, this time in Blanche's presence. He opens compartments, demands to know what is under the papers in the tin box, and then, snatching the love letters from Blanche's hands, starts to examine them. His curiosity knows no bounds. Isn't this a scene of violation, a possible foreshadowing of the so-called rape scene? Stanley is forcing Blanche to reveal things that she would not want to reveal. The love letters from Allan Grey are so precious to Blanche that she can't stand Stanley's hands touching them—"the touch of your hands insults them." "Everyone," she says, "has something he won't let others touch because of their intimate nature" (SND, 42). No matter how much Stanley pokes into these things, these "feminine" things, he will not understand them, and it is not just a matter of lack of education or difference in social class. Blanche occupies a different space, a space that will not be co-opted by the male order.

Blanche can be seen as attempting to stand outside the male power structure, as refusing to play the game according to its rules. She is condemned by the male order for attempting to step outside it. This becomes clear if we consider her in comparison to her sister, Stella. In his "Notebook for A Streetcar Named Desire," Elia Kazan argues that Stella has sold out:

> Stanley is her day and night. Her entire attention is to make herself pretty and attractive for Stanley, kill time till night. . . . She has sold herself out for a temporary solution. She's given up all hope, everything, just to live for Stanley's pleasures.[9]

Kazan concludes his discussion of Stella by quoting this note from Tennessee Williams,

> Gadge [Williams's nickname for Kazan]—I am a bit concerned over Stella in Scene One. It seems to me that she has two much vivacity, at times

she is bouncing around in a way that suggests a co-ed on a benzedrine kick. . . . Blanche is the quick one, light one. Stella is relatively slow and almost indolent. Blanche mentions her "Chinese philosophy"—the way she sits with her little hands folded like a cherub in a choir, etc. I think her natural passivity is one of the things that makes her acceptance of Stanley acceptable. She naturally "gives in," lets things slide, she does not make much of an effort.[10]

In her passivity, Stella has allowed herself to be appropriated by Stanley, and hence by the male order, by the patriarchy: the traditional economy of sexuality with the male as expropriator, the female as expropriated. We may agree with Kazan that "Stella will see Stanley differently following Blanche's calling her attention to her sell out," but nevertheless Stella, now with a baby as well as husband, will surely remain firmly entrenched within that traditional economy, within the family which Irigaray calls "the privileged locus of women's exploitation."[11] Although one may sense that Stella has other desires, that she is not fulfilled, Stanley and the male order in general would consider her to be behaving in an acceptable way, behaving as a woman should behave in their terms.

The notion that, in his home, as Stanley says, "Every man is a king!" (SND, 107) may have come down to us from the Greeks. There, the husband's authority, as Foucault points out, extended to "restriction of the wife's sexual activity which had to be completely within the conjugal relationship, with the husband as exclusive partner."[12] Furthermore, "[a] man's marriage did not restrict him sexually. . . . For while the woman belonged to the husband, the husband belonged only to himself."[13] All of this may have affected the way we see woman's desire today. Indeed, Luce Irigaray suggests that "woman's desire has doubtless been submerged by the logic that has dominated the West since the time of the Greeks."[14] Stella's decision to believe (or pretend to believe Stanley) at the end is a decision to believe or pretend to believe a lie. The decision is a reflection of patriarchal power. It demonstrates the power of the patriarchy to preserve the social order in a way that it considers to be in its best interest.

It is evident that for most of the characters in the play, in comparison to Stanley's speech, Blanche's speech is discredited; but the reasons for this are not clear. One may ask whether Stanley is believed because he speaks as a man and Blanche not believed because she speaks as a woman. Anca Vlasopolos argues that Stanley's ability to transform Blanche from "strong antagonist" to victim is assisted by "the conventions of social discourse that discredit her speech while valuing Stanley's."[15] Vlasopolos also suggests that "despite the fact that Blanche represents only an illusory threat to the Kowalski union while Stanley's rape has the power to destroy the marriage, the man's act is more easily forgiven than the female's desire." This "female's desire," however, remains undefined.

Not subject to a husband's control, Blanche's desire, unlike Stella's, seems unrestricted, and for the men it seems only too transparent. It may remind the reader of the desire of Elena, called variously "Elena of the Springs" and "Elena of the Desert" in *The Purification,* Williams's only verse-drama, published in *27 Wagons Full of Cotton and Other One-Act Plays* about three years before *A Streetcar Named Desire.* "Transparency," says the Son, "is a bad omen / in very young girls! / It makes flight / necessary / sometimes!" (27W, 34) The girl's desire "went beyond all fences" (27W, 35). It was a desire, according to the Son, that one "could certainly never—enclose" (27W, 35). The Rancher from Casa Rojo describes how he punishes Elena when he finds her with her brother:

> I looked for the coolness of springs
> in the woman's body?
> That finding none,
> or finding it being cut off—drained away
> at the source by the least suspected,
> I struck?
> And struck?
> And tore the false rock open?
>
> (27W, 58)

Although married, Elena maintained an incestuous relationship with her brother. Once again the patriarchy, this time represented by the Rancher, has to maintain the social order and so the woman, "the false rock," has to be torn open. Failing to control the woman's desire and sexual behavior, the man destroys her. Once again, men are describing female desire. They see her desire as insatiable, flowing like water in all directions, just as Stanley, based mainly on his supposed knowledge of her activities in Laurel, portrays Blanche's desire as insatiable. When the false rock is torn open or the lights of the world are switched on this is what the men think they find—the woman whose desire is insatiable, infinite.

The male order supposes that unlike Blanche's or Elena's, Stella's desire can be contained. It does not leap any fences. Stella has allowed herself to be owned, associated as a woman traditionally has been, with a place, the home, and now with reproduction and mothering. "[T]he man," says Irigaray, "by virtue of his effective participation in public exchanges has never been reduced to a simple reproductive function. The woman, for her part, owing to her seclusion in the 'home,' the place of private property, has long been nothing but a mother."[16] Blanche, on the other hand, is owned by nobody, and is not secluded in a "home" because she has no home. She is a person without a place or a space to call her own. In Irigaray's terms, Stella would be "the woman locked up in the house" and Blanche would be "the woman in the street."[17] Blanche is irrevocably displaced, and this "displacement," as Vlasopolos argues, "leaves her at a tremendous disadvantage when it comes to establishing her authority."[19]

Invoking "Marx's analysis of commodities as the elementary form of capitalist wealth," Irigaray argues that this "can be understood as an interpretation of women in so-called patriarchal societies."[19] For the patriarchy, then, a woman is a commodity and the next obvious question is what is this or that commodity worth?

> —just as in commodities, natural utility if overridden by the exchange function, so the properties of woman's body have to be suppressed and subordinated to the exigencies of its transformation into an object of circulation among men;
>
> —just as a commodity has no mirror it can use to reflect itself, so woman serves as reflection, as image of and for man, but lacks specific qualities of her own. Her value-invested form amounts to what man inscribes in and on its matter: that is, her body.[20]

Of course, both Blanche and Stella are concerned about how their bodies will receive favor in men's eyes. Irigaray, arguing that women "derives her price from her relation to the male sex, constituted as transcendental value: the phallus," says that "women no longer relate to each other except in terms of what they represent in men's desire,"[21] and this is particularly true, I think, of Blanche and Stella. Thus in scene 3, while the men play poker, the two women discuss the men (Stella draws attention to Stanley, her man; Blanche asks about Mitch, possibly her man to be) and in full view of the audience, change their clothes. Blanche removes her blouse and "stands in her pink silk brassiere and white skirt" (SND, 50) before slipping on "a dark red satin wrapper" (53). "Stella has removed her dress and put on a light blue satin kimono" (50).

Both women are well aware of themselves as objects of the male gaze. Elia Kazan says of Stella that "her entire attention is to make herself pretty and attractive for Stanley."[22] Stella herself is very much aware of her sister's need to be considered "pretty and attractive" by everyone, not just one person. In scene 2, Stella shows her awareness of Blanche's preoccupation as she (Stella) urges Stanley to "admire her dress and tell her she looks wonderful. That's important with Blanche. Her little weakness" (SND, 33). Blanche is obsessively concerned with her appearance, intent on presenting to the male the female that she believes he wants to see. "Hello Stanley," she declares in scene 2, "Here I am, all freshly bathed and scented, and feeling like a brand new human being!" Again she is changing her clothes: "Excuse me while I slip into my pretty new dress!" (37). The male gaze is not enough for her. She needs the gaze to be translated into words: "Would you think it possible that I was once considered to be— attractive?" (39).

Unlike Stella, Blanche has no maternal role to play in terms of actual motherhood, so her value in the economy suggested by Irigaray is dependent on her femininity:

> But in fact that "femininity" is a role, an image, a value, imposed upon women by male systems of representation. In this masquerade of femininity the woman loses herself, and loses herself by playing on her femininity. The fact remains that this masquerade requires an *effort* on her part for which she is not compensated. Unless her pleasure comes from being chosen as an object of consumption or of desire by masculine "subjects." And, moreover, how can she do otherwise without being "out of circulation."[23]

If Blanche, then, is to retain a reasonable value on the market, she has to play on femininity, or to be more precise, on "the masquerade of feminity." There is no doubt that this requires a great deal of effort. She confides in Stella, "I'm fading now! I don't know how much longer I can turn the trick" (SND, 79). There is also no doubt that she derives pleasure from being the object of desire, but surely her desire transcends the desire to be desired. Indeed, she has to act out "the masquerade of femininity" to avoid falling "out of circulation," but does this mean that she always surrenders herself to a desire that is not her own?

Arguing that a woman finds pleasure by "proxy," Irigaray main-tains that

> such pleasure is above all a masochistic prostitution of her body to a desire that is not her own, and it leaves her in a familiar state of dependency upon man. Not knowing what she wants, ready for anything, even asking for more, so long as he will "take" her as his object when he seeks his own pleasure. Thus she will not say what she herself wants; moreover she does not know, or no longer knows what she wants.[24]

Irigaray, of course, implies that this "desire that is not her own" is man's desire. She seems to assume that although men know their desire, women do not. In *A Streetcar Named Desire,* however, Blanche DuBois not only seems to know what she wants, but also says what she wants—so, for Irigaray, Blanche would be behaving as a woman unintimidated by the male desire for the masquerade. Perhaps this is what the men in *A Streetcar Named Desire,* particularly Mitch and Stanley, cannot tolerate. Furthermore, in addition to being the object of a man's sexual enjoyment, as the one who enjoys, in a sense, she becomes a man. She reverses the tradition of the man seeking the female—she becomes the seducer rather than the seduced—and to complicate matters even further she is the seducer of boys. The men realize that Blanche has sought pleasure, pleasure not in surrendering her body to a desire that is not her own, but in seeking to satisfy her "own" desire—and if that desire happens to be for seventeen-year-old blue-eyed boys and operates outside the marital scene, then she steps outside the traditional economy and becomes expropriator rather than expropriated.

Mitch tells Blanche, "Just give me a slap whenever I step out of bounds" (91), but Blanche, in seducing boys, is the one who steps "out of bounds." Stanley tells Stella that "there was an army camp near Laurel and [her] sister's was one of the places called 'Out of Bounds'" (100). Blanche, then, not only steps out of bounds, but is out of bounds. Since the loss of Belle Reve she has not had a place to call her own, but she does occupy a space, a space that is called "out of bounds." Unable to appropriate her, the phallocratic discourse pushes her to the margins in an attempt to exclude her, but she will not be excluded. As long as she remains desirable, the phallocratic discourse will try to appropriate her, and the men or boys will try to have her, but then of course, she can be seen as having them. Foucault suggests that in the Greek world there was a "dividing line" between

"the 'active actors' in the drama of pleasures and the 'passive actors.'"
The former were the men, "the subjects of sexual activity" and the
latter were "women, boys, slaves," "the objects of possible pleasure."[25]
Insofar as Blanche uses the boys for her "own" pleasure, then, she is
the "subject" rather than "object" and behaves not like a woman, a
boy, or a slave, but like a man.

The other way in which Blanche fails to behave like a woman as
the male order with its phallocratic discourse would have her behave
is not only that she speaks, but also that she speaks about her desire.
This is another way in which she separates herself from Stella. We
have already seen how quieter Stella is than Blanche. Later in the
play we see that if she does speak, her husband can shut her up. One
exception, of course, is during the poker night: when Stanley tells her
to "hush up," she replies calmly, "This is my house and I'll talk as
much as I want to" (SND, 51). This could be one of the things that
triggers Stanley's violent behavior later in the scene. Not only does
she speak, but she challenges the crucial notion of male ownership
and economic domination, so Stanley must put his (the) woman in
her "place." Generally, however, Stella keeps quiet, and unlike
Blanche, she does not discuss her desire in front of the men. Nobody,
however, can stop Blanche from speaking. In the end, she has to leave
Elysian Fields; but in the madhouse, doubtless, she will continue to
speak, to speak about her desire.

Like the blank in her name, Blanche remains open. Although pene-
trated and marked, she is never really possessed, and never silenced.
She will express her desire(s). Instead of yielding completely to the
dominant male economy of desire, as the silent Stella has done, she
attempts to stand outside it. Stella's desire falls neatly into the space
that the masculine order with its phallocratic discourse has allocated
for it. Blanche's desire, on the other hand, although it will sometimes
occupy that space, will also occupy the space outside that offered by
the masculine order for the feminine and will occupy the space that
the masculine order itself occupies; for the text makes possible, as I
have already pointed out, a reading of Blanche not only as a woman
but also as a man. In both cases, she is marginalized. As a woman she
is marginalized simply by virtue of being a woman. As a man she is
marginalized for seeking out the boy as the object of pleasure. I am not
saying that Blanche's desire occupies a space outside the phallocratic
discourse, for as Irigaray has suggested there may be no such position;
I am saying that within that discourse Blanche occupies the space

assigned for the feminine and the space of the masculine that is doing the assigning. The reading of Blanche simply as a woman ignores the play of gender and sexuality, which we also saw in the play of her name. As a woman she is marginalized by this phallocratic discourse. As a man for whom boys are the object of her desire, in other words as a homosexual, Blanche is marginalized again.

The purpose of what may seem like a long digression on female desire has been to show the difficulty of coming up with any reading that assigns themes, as Adler attempts to do, in relation to the supposed opposition between Blanche and Stanley. In particular, Adler errs when he puts "desire" in Stanley's world. Why should desire be put in Stanley's world when Blanche's desire, as I have argued, may be seen as occupying more space than either the men's or the womens' because it can occupy both worlds? Also, it is not just a question of proving Adler wrong, for I may be seen as unfairly picking on one or two dichotomies in his extensive list. The important additional point, for my purposes, is that there may be a parallel between the space occupied by desire and the space of the signature, for both exist on the margin of the text and both attempt to connect inside to outside.

Tennessee Williams, then, signs through the desire named in the title, which cannot be reduced to either Stanley's desire or Blanche's desire. Although Williams himself has emphasized his own affinity with Blanche and others have been quick to recognize this affinity, there is also an affinity between Williams and the character generally regarded as Blanche's polar opposite, Stanley Kowalski. Indeed, when Williams claims, "I am afraid that I don't find it easy to identify with these Stanley Kowalski's and so forth" (CN, 117), he himself is not denying that he can identify with Stanley to some extent.

Discussing the relationship between Williams and his characters, Mike Steen suggests "all his characters are a bit of him. It's astounding that when you really get to know him you recognize all these different characters inside him, summed up into one severely complex character of his actual being. It's amazing, I think to see the aspects of Stanley Kowalski in him as well as those of Blanche DuBois and Alma Winemiller, Valentine Xavier, or Alexandra del Lago, or Flora Goforth. . . . You'd think, 'How can a person have that many selves?'"[26] In fact, in talking about his characters in general, Williams writes, "I have to identify with the character in some way, or the character is not real. I sometimes wish that my writing was less personal."[27]

Parallels between Blanche, Williams, and Stanley include their sexual voraciousness. They may all also be thought of as being competitive. As I suggested in chapter 1, Williams has to be competitive in order to survive as a playwright. Stanley relishes the competition involved in a game of poker, enjoying his success in the game of poker, perhaps almost as much as in his successes with women. Blanche tends to compete with Stella.

In certain respects, Williams seems more like Stanley than like Blanche. At times Williams and Stanley demonstrate a similar sense of humor. Stanley's story about the bottle top, which concerns a cousin who used to open beer bottles with his teeth, but who eventually broke his teeth off at a wedding party typifies the kind of humor shared by Williams himself. Stanley's story reminds me of the story of the old man dying after falling asleep with the cigar in his mouth, a story that Windham says Tennessee much enjoyed.[28] Both Stanley and Williams can be very cruel. Stanley's cruelty manifests itself, for example, in the birthday supper scene when he presents Blanche with a one-way ticket to Laurel. Many of the people closest to Williams have testified to his moments of cruelty, his suddenly turning on them for no apparent reason. Williams never forgave himself for once saying to his sister, Rose, "I hate the sight of your ugly old face!" (MS, 122), and used to cry when telling the story of how, when he and Rose were very young, "he would tug at her ringlets, shouting, 'Ding, dong, ding, dong!'" and would later ask Maria St. Just, "How could I have been so cruel!"[29] Donald Windham provides detailed personal testimony concerning Williams's vacillation between "sensitivity and kindness" and "callousness and cruelty."[30]

In discussing competitiveness, cruelty, or desire in *A Streetcar Named Desire*, though, we are involved in the thematic, but like Derrida, Williams has expressed a frustration with thematicism:

> Often I'm asked if my pessimism, my characters, my violent scenes are not a reflection of the chaos of our world. Well, sometimes I oblige my questioners with a cosmic answer, but really I'm fed up with pontificating. You're trapped into making a statement that sounds pretentious. It's all very simple. I write because I love writing. It's what I know how to do, and I work every day. What else is there?[31]

The signature in its second modality is able to stop short of the leap to theme and thus sidestep the problem of referentiality.

Derrida pays particular attention to the possibility or impossibility of referentiality in "The Double Session" where he considers a text entitled "Mimique" that is part of Mallarmé's "Crayonné au théâtre," which involves a discussion of a mime by Paul Margueritte called *Pierrot Murderer of His Wife*. It is the mime that alerts Mallarmé and Derrida to the inadequacy not only of thematicism but also of any approach that stays within the confines of the mere "word." The thematic approach to a text takes off from the word, but why, say Derrida and Mallarmé, should the signifier only lie in the word as a whole? What about signifiers within the word itself? "Thematicism," argues Derrida, "necessarily leaves out of account the formal, phonic, or graphic affinities that do not have the shape of a word, the calm unity of the verbal sign." Derrida claims that "Thematicism as such necessarily ignores the play that takes the word apart, cutting it up and putting the pieces to work 'on the basis of some contingency.'" Although Derrida emphasizes and shares Mallarmé's interest in "the possibilities inherent in the *word*," he recognizes that "these possibilities are not primarily nor exclusively those of a body proper, a carnal unit . . . it is a play of articulations splitting up that body or reinscribing it within sequences it can no longer control" (DS, 255).[32]

It is possible, then, that in Williams's text(s) the signature event is played off in relation, not simply to his characters—for example, Blanche and Stanley—but also in relation to the phonic signifiers *bl* and *st*. Williams's scholars have already begun to show a concern not just for the words but for the phonic signifiers within certain words. Ortrun Zuber, for example, makes the astute observation that in *A Streetcar Named Desire* "the sound sign establishes a clear relation between Stanley and the 'Streetcars,' hence the title of the play."[33] Zuber also notes that "for a German audience it is much more difficult to detect the significance of this sign." Zuber does not, however, and this is not intended to be a criticism of Zuber, avail himself of the opportunity to explore further manifestations of this "sound sign" or "phonic signifier" *st* that presumably is the connection which he sees or hears between Stanley and Streetcar.

As well as Stanley, Stella and Steve had names that begin with *st*. The word *straight* begins with *st* and so does the word *stud*. Mitch, as we have seen, says to Blanche, "I was fool enough to believe you was straight"; to which Blanche replies, "Who told you I wasn't 'straight'" (Williams's quotation marks; SND, 117). In observing the quotation marks round "straight," we see that the word draws attention to itself. In Kazan's movie version of the play, the word *straight* receives even more emphasis because Blanche replies to Mitch's question by herself asking a question, "What's straight? A line can be straight or a street. But the heart of a human being?"[34]

Thus, although hardly a straight one, a line can be traced from the street in the title, *Streetcar,* to this street running through Stanley ("survivor of the *stone* age" [72]), Stella ("*Stella, Stella* for *Star*"), Steve, and everyone else in a story that ends with the word *stud*: "This game is seven-card *stud*" (142). Having linked the word *stud* to "the male atmosphere," Zuber reads this last sentence of the play as "indicating that the game of men will go on."[35] I may be tempted to go along with this reading and further speculate that it is, in fact, a victory not just for the men but for the *st* world which may incorporate the world of the men. The problem with this argument, however, is that if we recall, for example, that Stella's name places her in the *st* world, then, we must remember that the *st* world is not reducible to the so-called maculine order.

Furthermore, one may suspect that the existing male power structure is maintained when Stella says "I couldn't believe her *story* and go on living with *Stanley*" (emphasis added; SND, 133). This may be to assume, however, that Blanche's world, let us designate it the world of the *bl*, is neatly opposed to the world of the *st*. But, we should remember that Blanche, according to a logic developed earlier, is also a man. The phonic signifiers *st* and *bl* cannot, therefore, be thought of in terms of a straightforward masculine/feminine opposition. We may also recall our observations on the name of the country estate, *Belle* Reve. The gender problem there also affects the *bl*. The masculine *reve* prevents a simple designation of the *bl* as feminine.

My suggestion that Blanche exists on the edge between the masculine order and the space assigned for the feminine may still apply, but these spaces can now be incorporated into the *bl* versus *st* opposition, an opposition that may be more fruitful because it can incorporate so much more. While not undermining any of the suggestions that have been made concerning gender and sexual issues, the *bl/st* opposition takes us beyond them by incorporating other issues. Sexuality now falls under the category of *bl/st*.

Like the *st*, the *bl* obviously occurs in contexts other than sexual contexts. Through the phonic signifier *bl*, Blanche is connected to the color blue. Although Blanche is clearly fascinated with the color blue, as we have already seen, she is also, through her name, through her attire when she first enters the play, and through other means linked to the color white. Notice that she brings the two colors, white (*blanche*) and blue together in her suggestion that Stella's baby's eyes should "be like candles, like two *blue* candles lighted in *a white* cake!" (emphasis added; SND, 109). She also brings the two colors together in her desire to be "buried at sea sewn up in a clean *white* sack and dropped overboard—at noon—in the *blaze* of summer—and into an ocean as *blue* as . . . my first lover's eyes" (emphasis added, 136).

At the end of *A Streetcar Named Desire*, Blanche wears a Della Robia blue jacket, which she compares to "the blue of the robe of the old Madonna pictures" (135). The color blue links her to *The Glass Menagerie*'s Laura, who is nicknamed "Blue Roses," and to *Battle of Angels*' Myra, whose dress is "ecstasy blue" (BA, 202). It also links her to Don Quixote, whose first words in *Camino Real* are "Blue is the color of distance! . . . Blue is also the color of nobility . . . . Blue is also the color of nobility, and that's why an old knight should have somewhere about him a bit of blue ribbon" (CR, 2). It also links her to *The Purification*'s Elena, who leaves behind a space which is "Blue— / Blue— / Immortally blue" (27W, 59).[36]

The *bl* then brings together these marginal individuals and links them also to the *blues* musicians excluded from the mainstream and, therefore, in *A Streetcar Named Desire* always playing round the corner. There is also an obvious connection between blue and blues. Paul Oliver puts it like this, "You have a tough way in life—that makes you blue. That's when you start to sing the blues—when you've got the blues."[37] Blue also brings together "the blue piano" of *A Streetcar Named Desire* and "the blue guitar" of *Ten Blocks on the Camino Real*. Williams has even signed himself as blue. He ends a letter to Marie St. Just, "Devotedly, your blue fish, 10."[38]

The *bl* may be seen as assigning a place for marginalia—not only women and homosexuals, but also rootless wanderers, poets, blues musicians, the chronically shy (Laura—"Blue Roses"), the fragile (Laura whose image is "the lovely fragility of glass" [GM 9] and mothlike Blanche [SND 15]), and those with a chronic need for alcohol (Blanche of Drink).

Other words that begin in *bl* include the words *blood* and *bleed*. These, in turn, are linked to blue in this passage from a short story entitled "The Field of Blue Children" where Homer, a poet, and Myra, a college girl, wander into a field:

They were both kneeling in the *blue* flowers, facing each other. The wind *blew* her loose hair into his face. He raised both hands and brushed it back over her forehead and as he did so his hands slipped down behind the back of her forehead fastened there and drew her head toward him until her mouth was pressed against his, tighter and tighter, until her teeth pressed painfully against her upper lip and she tasted the salt taste of blood. She gasped and let her mouth fall open and then she lay back against the whispering blue flowers. (emphasis added; CS, 77)

In *A Streetcar Named Desire,* the *bl* brings similar references to "blood" and "blue" together in Blanche's outburst in scene 1: "But you are the one that abandoned Belle Reve, not I! I stayed and fought for it, *bl*ed for it, almost died for it! . . . I, I, I took the *bl*ows in my face and on my body!"—as she says these things, "the music of the 'blue piano' gets louder" (emphasis added; SND, 26) A series of signifiers is thus established, running through Blanche's name to blue, blues, blood, bleed, and blows. We should also not forget the translation of the French word *blanche* into English as "blank."

Finding a "blank" in Mallarmé's texts, Derrida argues that "the blank is the polysemic totality of everything white or blank plus the writing site . . . where such a totality is produced. . . ." He maintains that "it is out of the question that we should erect such a representative—for example the whiteness of the page of writing into the fundamental signified or signifier in the series" (DS, 252). It is difficult to deny the logic here, so although our starting point for the *st/bl* opposition was the opposition between Stanley and Blanche, we cannot privilege them as fundamental signifieds in their respective chains. As a signifier, Stanley may be no more important than Stella, Steve, straight, stud, stone, and story in that series; and as a signifier Blanche may be no more important than blue, blues, blood, bleed, blows, and blank in that series. It may not be the case that the two chains are rigorously divided. Stanley, for example, may wear *bl*ue jeans, or the *bl*ues may be associated with *St*ella rather than *Bl*anche; but nevertheless, it is difficult to deny that a clear pattern is established; and the *bl* and the *st* offer themselves up as more important signifying structures than any of the individual links in their respective chains.

Although it is not necessary to formulate an exact inventory of either the *bl* or the *st*, my analysis has concentrated primarily on *A Streetcar Named Desire,* and we may wonder if the *bl/st* opposition can function as a signature event in other Williams texts. As I look through the titles of Williams's plays, suddenly *Suddenly Last Summer* catches my eye, Suddenly La*ST* Summer. Here I find the *st*, but I find that the two letters are at the end of a word rather than at the beginning. They are the last letters and not the first. I ask myself whether they are pronounced in the same way at the end of "Last" as they are at the beginning of "Streetcar." And what of the *bl*? Is the *bl* in *Bl*anche pronounced like the *bl* in Vena*bl*e? The difficulties here suggest that it is necessary to move away from thinking of the *bl* and the *st* as simply phonic signifiers. I am reminded of the passage in *Glas* where Derrida seems frustrated with his *gl*.

> I do not say either the signifier GL, or the phoneme GL, or the grapheme GL. Mark would be better, if the word were well understood, or if one's ears were open to it; not even mark then.
>   It is also imprudent to advance or set GL swinging in the masculine or feminine, to write or articulate it in capital letters. That has no identity, sex, gender, makes no sense, is neither a definite whole nor a part detached from a whole
>   gl remain(s) gl (GL, 119b)

Certainly I can no longer consider *st* and *bl* as simply phonemes or phonic signifiers. Perhaps I could call them marks—marks on or in the body of Williams's writing. One could employ other terms suggested by Derrida, "consonants without vowels," or "'sounding' syllables," or "non-vocalizable letters" (GL 120b), but why not simply call them *bl* and *st*?

Reading *Suddenly Last Summer* and recognizing *bl* and *st* as its subject, as in *A Streetcar Named Desire,* I find many references to "*st*ory." In the opening scene, Mrs. Venable tells the Doctor, "I haven't heard the girl's story except indirectly in a watered down version" (SLS, 24), and this is in the context of the Doctor's question, "Did your son have a—well—what kind of a personal, well, private life did—" (23). The story in *Suddenly Last Summer,* like the story in *A Streetcar Named Desire,* has to do with a character's sexual past. Mrs. Venable tries to ensure that the story of her son Sebastian's sexuality and death is not heard. She wants "the fantastic story," "that horrible story," "the crazy story," to be erased, and so at the end of the play when Catherine has told the story, Mrs. Venable screams, "Cut this hideous story out of her brain!" (93). Spoken by the Doctor, the last line of *Suddenly Last Summer,* "I think we ought to at least consider the possibility that the girl's story could be true" (93), provides us with the last reference to story-telling. The Doctor has insisted all along that Catherine tell the truth: "You will tell the true story. . . . The absolutely true story. No lies, nothing not spoken. Everything told exactly" (70). *Suddenly Last Summer* is a play that is as concerned with questions of truth and falsehood as is A *Streetcar Named Desire.* In scene 3, George and his mother, Mrs. Holly, urge Catherine not to tell the story:

> *George.* You can't tell such a story to civilized people in a civilized up-to-date country!
> *Mrs. Holly.* Cathy, why, why, why!—did you invent such a tale?
> *Catherine.* But, Mother, I DIDN'T invent it. I know it's a hideous story but it's a true story of our time and the world we live in.
>
> (SLS, 47)

This "true story of our time" involves homosexuality. Once again it is through a woman's discourse that a space is opened up to accommodate homosexuality. Once again, the homosexual is only present through words. The name appears but not the person.

Names are on Mrs. Venable's mind in the opening scene as she explains to the Doctor that the Latin names written on tags attached to the plants in Sebastian's garden have faded. This talk of names leads to a discussion of her son's name. She tells the Doctor that "Sebastian had no public name as a poet, he didn't want one, he refused to have one. He *dreaded, abhorred!*—false values that come from being publicly known, from fame" (Williams's emphasis, 13).[39] Mrs. Venable can be seen as placing her son in the *st* world, the "straight" world. One way she does this is by insisting to the Doctor,

> before you hear whatever you're going to hear from the girl when she gets here. My son, Sebastian, was chaste. Not c-h-a-s-e-d! Oh, he was chased in that way of spelling it too, we had to be very fleet-footed I can tell you with his looks and his charm, to keep ahead of pursuers, every kind of pursuer!—I mean he was c-h-a-s-t-e!—Chaste. (SLS, 24)

Here she literally insists on the *st,* on the spelling with "*ste*" not "sed." In insisting on Sebastian's chastity, she is insisting on his whiteness. Of course, he used to dress in white. On the day of his death, according to Catherine, "Sebastian was white as the weather. He had on a spotless white silk Shantung suit and a white silk tie and a white panama and white shoes, white—white lizard skin—pumps! He . . . kept touching his face and his throat here and there with a white silk and popping little white pills in his mouth" (SLS, 82). As Catherine's account continues, the repetitions of the word white become almost incantational: "It was all white outside. White hot, a blazing white hot, hot blazing white . . . As if a huge white bone had caught on fire in the sky and blazed so bright it was white and turned the sky and every-thing under the sky white with it!" The confused doctor queries the word "White" (89), but Catherine insists "Yes—white" (90). There is a connection between Sebastian and Blanche here in terms of con-cealing or whitewashing sexual history. Blanche, whose name, as we have seen, means white hides her sexual history beneath the white apparel with which she enters *A Streetcar Named Desire*. Sebastian in *Suddenly Last Summer* also wears white but rather than concealing his own sexual history, that history is concealed, glossed over by his mother. We recall that at the beginning of *Suddenly Last Summer*, Mrs Venable insisted on the word "chaste." In doing so, she totally misrepresents her son, for both she and later Catherine acted as pro-curers of young men for Sebastian.

Like Blanche, Sebastian, in fact, moves between the two worlds, the world of the *st* and the world of the *bl*. Like the sky under which he dies that "blazed so bright it was white," Sebastian, although not present on stage, *bl*azes white. His whiteness places him in the *bl* world, of which he is by virtue of his last name, Vena*bl*e, already a part: Sebastian Vena*bl*e. So, this character who, I repeat, never appears on stage functions in a similar way to Blanche, floating between the two discourses, not really a part of either, but living on the border, on the edge.

As an unambiguously homosexual character and as a poet, Sebastian may be more like Williams than Blanche is like Williams. In fact, the actress Ann Meacham maintained that Tennessee Williams himself was the model for Sebastian and that "in this play, he accused himself of 'devouring' others by buying sex and by paying for counterfeit emotion."[40] According to Catherine, Sebastian at a certain point in his life decided to seek out *bl*onds. "—We were *going* to blonds, blonds were next on the menu. . . . Cousin Sebastian said he was famished for blonds, he was fed up with the dark ones and was famished for blonds. All the travel brochures he picked up were advertisements of the blond northern countries" (Williams's emphasis; SLS, 39). This may remind us of a letter that Williams sent to Donald Windham informing him that "after two months in Italy he was getting an appetite for northern blonds, since he was tired of the Romans who were mostly dark."[41]

One of the beauties of the name Sebastian Venable is that it contains the *bl* and the *st*. I repeat, however, that Williams is not one of his characters. In terms of the *bl/st* opposition, the signature event can be seen as played off, not only in relation to say *Bl*anche and *St*anley, but also and perhaps most significantly in relation to *Seba*stian Vena*bl*e.

Like Blanche, Sebastian is also connected to the *bl*ank and to the color *bl*ue. Each summer he writes one poem in "the Blue Jay note-book," "a school composition book with a Blue Jay trademark" (SLS, 74–75). In scene 4, Mrs. Venable produces the notebook that was sent back from Cabeza de Lobo along with Sebastian's personal effects:

> *Mrs. Venable.* This is important.... Here it is, here! [*She holds up a notebook and leafs swiftly through the pages.*] Title? 'Poem of Summer,' and the date of the summer—1935. After that: *what? Blank pages, blank pages,* nothing but *nothing!*—last summer. . . .
> *Doctor.* What's that got to do with—?
> *Mrs. Venable.* His destruction? I'll tell you. A poet's vocation is something that rests on something as thin and fine as the web of a spider, Doctor.
> (Williams's emphasis; SLS, 75–76)

Like all writers, Sebastian must have been faced with the blank page. Sebastian's external appearance, the weather, and so on, can now, therefore, all be thought of as "white as a yet unwritten page."[42] There is also a correspondence between the blank pages and Sebastian's de-sire for boys, which grows and grows. As time goes by, "the empty Blue Jay notebook got bigger and bigger, so big it was big and empty as that empty blue sea and sky" (SLS, 81). Sebastian's desire blazes. Catherine insists that on the fateful day of his death "it was one of those white *bl*azing days in Cabeza de Lobo, not a *bl*azing hot *bl*ue one, but a *bl*azing hot white one" (my emphasis; SLS, 82). Whether white *(blanche)* or blue *(bl*ue), this is the quintessential *bl* discourse, the discourse of excessive desire. I am reminded of Artaud's comment, "An iron can be heated until it is white, so it can be said that every-thing excessive is white."[43] Finally, having chased and used the boys for his own sexual gratification, Sebastian is chased by, torn apart by, and literally devoured by the boys. Catherine's narrative ends with this unforgettable image,

> There wasn't a sound any more, there was nothing to see but Sebastian, what was left of him, that looked like a big white-paper-wrapped bunch of red roses had been *torn, thrown, crushed!*—against that blazing white wall. (Williams's emphasis; SLS, 92)

Williams himself is dead. As he signs his texts he dies. "When I sign, I am already dead," says Derrida, "I hardly have the time to sign that I am already dead. . . . The structure of the 'signature' event carries my death in that event" (GL, 19b). Having traced Williams's stylistic signature, however, from the *bl*/*st* opposition in *A Streetcar Named Desire,* we are in a position to observe it once again in Catherine's closing statement. Williams is scattered through his corpus through this play of *bl*'s and *st*'s. Williams's signature may be found in the *st* discourse that links Sebastian to his namesake St. Sebastian and to Stanley, the Streetcar, and Stella. Sebastian's death occurs near a "*st*eep white *st*reet" (emphasis added; SLS, 91). Williams's signature may also be found in the "white street," the "white paper," the "*bl*az-ing white wall," and even in the image of the "red roses" suggestive of Sebastian's *bl*ood. Pieces of Sebastian's body find their way "into those gob*bl*ing fierce empty *bl*ack mouths of theirs" (emphasis added; SLS 92), just as pieces of Williams's signature find their way into the once empty, white, virginal pages of Williams's texts and long ago the limbs of Orpheus were scattered across the Thracian fields.

I should emphasize that I am not suggesting that *bl* versus *st* could possibly be Tennessee Williams's actual or nominal signature, in the sense that he would have used it as his autograph or to sign checks. It is a stylistic signature established by means of a textual logic. Al-though the structure of this signature may be independent of any signifying intention, it does seem appropriate that Tennessee Wil-liams's signature be dual because the man himself was so paradoxical. Robert Rice claims

> He is obviously one of the most trusting, suspicious, generous, egocentric, helpless, self-reliant, fearful, courageous, absentminded, observant, mod-est, vain, withdrawn, gregarious, puritanical, Bohemian, angry, mild, un-sure self-confident men in the U.S.[44]

Donald Windham quotes Williams's own observation in *Memoirs,* "Consistency, thy name is not Tennessee!" and argues that

> There is probably not an episode described in the "Memoirs" that did not happen at some time, to some one, in some way, but more likely than not to a different person, at a different time, with different details. Curtain after curtain of ambivalence has descended in his life. Self-portrait after self-portrait has intervened in his plays. And the same qualities that make Tennessee a good dramatist make him an impossible documenter.[45]

In *Lost Friendships* Windham elaborates on this ambivalence:

> Each of his traits was balanced, like the evenly weighed pans of a scale, by its opposite. He was ordinary in Montaigne's sense: bashful and bold, chaste and lascivious, talkative and taciturn, tough and delicate, clever and stupid, surly and affable, truthful and lying.[46]

Nevertheless, I have found some consistency in the *bl/st* opposition inscribed within Williams's texts. In looking for Williams's signature in terms of this opposition I have tried to make sense, but the play in Williams's texts must include the notion of play in terms of the opposition of *bl* versus *st*, and so the *bl* cannot always represent the margin, the world of women and homosexuals, any more than the *st* can always represent the male world or the "straight" world. The themes established by the *bl* may not be rigorously divided from those established by the *st*. One may also question whether the *bl* and *st* as signifiers are any more important than, for example, the semic units *blanche, anche, bois,* and so on, found in Blanche's name? Furthermore, isn't the whole idea of a dual signature a typical gesture of the phallocratic discourse that relies on oppositions? Irigaray asks, "How can we speak so as to escape from their compartments, their schemas, their distinctions and oppositions: virginal/deflowered, pure/impure, innocent/experienced. . . . How can we shake off the chains of these terms, free ourselves from their categories, rid ourselves of their names?"[47]

The idea, not only of oppositions but also of choosing between oppositions, is suggested in the epigraph that Williams uses for *A Streetcar Named Desire*:

> And so it was I entered the broken world
> To trace the visionary company of love, its voice
> An instant in the wind (I know not whither hurled)
> But not for long to hold each desperate choice.
> "The Broken Tower" by HART CRANE

Although at times the opposition that I have suggested between *bl* and *st* may constitute a powerful signifying structure in Williams's texts, the *bl* and the *st* can also be regarded as not constituting an opposition at all. Just because a person seems to have contradictory elements in his character, this is hardly a sound argument for saying that his signature must embody an opposition. If that were the case, perhaps we would all have dual signatures? Just as Tennessee Williams's signature is not reducible to Blanche or to Stanley, it is not reducible to the opposition between Blanche and Stanley or to themes that seem to hover around their respective worlds. Tennessee Williams's signature is not reducible, for example, to any simple categories of sexuality.

Derrida has questioned "the line of cleavage between the two sexes" and has wondered why anatomy should be "the final recourse?" (EO, 181). He speculates about a relationship "beyond the opposition feminine/masculine, beyond bisexuality as well, beyond homosexuality and heterosexuality." In this poignant passage Derrida dreams of the displacement of overarching dualisms:

> I would like to believe in the multiplicity of sexually marked voices. I would like to believe in the masses, this indeterminable number of blended voices, this mobile of non-identified sexual marks whose choreography can carry, divide, multiply the body of each "individual," whether he be classified as "man" or as "woman" according to the criteria of usage. Of course, it is not impossible that desire for a sexuality without number can still protect us, like a dream, from an implacable destiny which immures everything for life in the figure 2. (EO, 184)

Of course, Tennessee Williams was obsessed with sexuality; but his life was not just a matter of sexuality, and his signature is also not reducible to sexuality. Indeed, how could it be reducible to an opposition between the sexes or between homosexuality and heterosexuality when there is the possibilitty of "a sexuality without number"? Indeed, the objection to the idea of oppositions, to thinking in terms of "the figure 2" may lead one to question all oppositions and not just oppositions in terms of gender or sexuality.

The stylistic opposition between *bl* and *st* that I have explored is not only irreducible to any categories of gender or sexuality, but also to any other thematicism. The play of the *bl* and the *st*, however, does constitute a significant moment of style, and this may be the closest that I have been able to get in terms of discovering Tennessee Williams's "inimitable idiom." It is possible that this signature in its second modality, this play of *bl* and *st*, that I have discovered first in *A Streetcar Named Desire* and then *Suddenly Last Summer* will always be found in Williams's texts. Throughout Williams's corpus, we may discover the same kind of stylistic signature, the same suggestions of opposition, although perhaps in some cases the suggestions of opposition involved in this modality of the signature may be represented by other letters.

*   *   *

Williams's Signature in Its Third Modality

In *The Ear of the Other: Otobiography, Transference, Translation*, Derrida considers the subject of play when discussing Freud's analysis of child's play. Like Freud, Derrida refuses to believe that "play is insignificant, that it is purely a game" (EO, 67). Derrida does not adopt the view that he labels "obscurantist" which says, "Okay, that's a game. It's gratuitous, play for the sake of play; it means nothing, it's pure expenditure" (68). Instead, he expresses his interest in play that is potentially meaningful and is "no longer the play of someone who plays." Derrida argues that "Philosophy has always made play into an activity, the activity of a subject manipulating objects." For Derrida, subjects are manipulated and are not themselves manipulating. Thus, he is drawn to a kind of play that flies in the face of traditional philosophy but may consequently be "very risky" (69).

Commentators have been quick to criticize Derrida's penchant for play. Madison, for example, argues that "Derrida joyfully embraces a 'Nietzschean' notion of play, a groundless and aimless play in which all standards and distinctions are meaningless, a form of play which rules out in advance any notion of 'progress' (progression) in which meaning is endlessly deferred in an endless supplementarity."[48] Surely, it is difficult to see how this argument could be substantiated. Derrida would certainly not agree that his use of play precludes any possible progress. He admits that it entails a risk, but surely the risk is worth taking precisely because it may lead to something, something inaccessible through traditional philosophy.

Thus, rather than dismissing play as traditional philosophy has done as something not serious, something that can be conveniently placed on the margin, Derrida finds play potentially very useful. We have seen that an appreciation of play is indispensable when considering both intertextuality and the second modality of the signature, and so it should come as no surprise to see that play is also characteristic of the third modality of the signature. This third modality involves the play of a *mise en abyme* structure. I suggest that this *mise en abyme* structure occurs in *A Streetcar Named Desire* in terms of the relation between the poker-playing scenes and the outer play. Paying attention to the apparent placement of the game of poker within the play, *A Streetcar Named Desire,* enables us to locate Williams's signature in terms of the work of writing itself.

Although Williams himself has argued that the idea for *A Streetcar Named Desire* began with an image of a woman sitting looking out of a window, it has also been suggested that at one time, Williams had only card scenes from which to develop the rest of the play.[49] In *The Kindness of Strangers,* Donald Spoto tells us that Williams tried to learn how to play poker during the New York run of *The Glass Menagerie.* Randy Echols said that at that time, "Tennessee wanted to learn how to play poker. He invited some of the crew from the play to his hotel room, provided cards and chips and liquor and foods, and then he went from player to player taking notes. We found out only later what he was doing and why he needed to learn" (KS, 118). One can imagine the playwright scurrying around the table and writing down phrases that would appear in the play: "Anything wild this deal?" "One-eyed jacks are wild" (SND, 45); "Drew to an inside straight and made it, by God!" (131); "This game is seven-card stud" (142). Williams, then, was doing research for the work in progress, *A Streetcar Named Desire,* which at that time was called *Blanche's Chair in the Moon,* but whose title was soon changed to *The Poker Night.* According to Spoto, the play that was eventually to become *A Streetcar Named Desire* "had only card scenes; there was considerable atmosphere and dramatic tension, but the narrative was undeveloped" (KS, 118). The outer play of *A Streetcar Named Desire,* then, may have developed around this inner play, this game of cards.

Although the play may have grown out of these poker scenes, the relationship between the card playing and the rest of the play should not be seen merely diachronically, that is simply in terms of the evolution of the play, for there is also clearly a synchronic relationship. The actual game in the play, stud poker, can be seen as commenting on the play that surrounds and includes it. According to Roger Caillois, game playing involves at least four elements: competition *(agon),* chance *(alea),* simulation (mimicry), and vertigo *(ilinx).* [50]

The nature of the game of poker is, in fact, foregrounded at the beginning of *A Streetcar Named Desire*'s final scene:

Stanley. Drew to an inside straight and made it, by God.
Pablo. Maldita sea tu suerte!
Stanley. Put it in English, greaseball.
Pablo. I am cursing your rutting luck.
Stanley [prodigiously elated]. You know what luck is? Luck is believing
  you're lucky. Take at Solerno. I believed I was lucky. I figured that 4
  out of 5 would not come through but I would . . . and I did. I put that
  down as a rule. To hold front position in this rat race you've got to
  believe you are lucky.
Mitch. You . . . you . . . you . . . Brag. . . . brag . . . bull . . . bull.

(SND, 131)

No matter how much Stanley brags ("brag" incidentally is the name
of a British card game that is equivalent to poker) about believing he
is lucky, the outcome of the game is influenced by chance. Pablo's
cursing of Stanley's "rutting luck" can be read as a reference to Stanley's success not only with cards but also with women. As we move
outward from the card game to the outer play that encases it, provides
it, if you will, with a home, we can see that the card players, Stanley,
Steve, Pablo, and Mitch are not the only players; Blanche and Stella,
as I said earlier, can be seen as competing for Stanley; Blanche and
Stanley can be seen as competing for Stella, for her affection, loyalty,
and support. Any one who has experienced the thrill of poker or just
been around a poker game where a lot of money was at stake, will
also know that vertigo, "the sense of giddiness which humans find
both alarming and attractive" is also a factor. Although not actually
playing poker, Blanche and Stella are caught up in this giddiness.
Blanche, in particular, seems constantly on the verge of fainting.

Simulation, which for Caillois, included "all forms of impersonation,
of becoming an illusory person and behaving accordingly" is another
factor.[51] In stud poker everything depends on your first card, the one
that is dealt face down and that you alone are allowed to look at. The
best players are those whose behavior leads you to believe that their
hands are good, but not quite as good as your own, with the result
that you will go on putting money in the pot, all of which will eventually be lost. Alternatively, they may be able to convince you that their
hand is very good, causing you to stack your hand when, in fact, your
hand turns out to be stronger than theirs. The trick, then, is to pretend
that you have quite a good hand when, in fact, it is a very good one
or to pretend that you have a great hand when, in fact, you really
have nothing at all—and get away with it. During the betting, if you

wager a lot of money, this could mean one of two things: either you are very confident that you have the winning hand or you are bluffing and simply trying to scare away the opposition. If you wager a lot of money only when you have a good hand, people will get the idea that you do not bluff, and your play will become predictable. The great poker player, however, is unpredictable: he is the great master of simulation, the master of pretense. He appears very confident when he is really not confident at all, and he appears very anxious when he is really very confident. Stanley may be right when he says you have to believe you are lucky, but the trick is not to let the other know what you are thinking. You have to be a master of the art of simulation.

When we look carefully at *A Streetcar Named Desire,* it is not difficult to see how the language of the card-playing scenes links those scenes to the rest of the play. Take, for example, the notion of the wild card. At the beginning of scene 3, "The Poker Night," Steve says, "Anything wild this deal?" (SND, 45). The thing about the wild card is that it can assume a value different to its ordinary value. Although it looks like an ordinary card, once it has been declared to be the wild card, it can function as any other card—any card that suits your hand. Thus, it can dispense with the role that it usually plays and play a great variety of other roles. Surely, Blanche may be regarded as the wild card in the game of *A Streetcar Named Desire.* This is not because her behavior leads characters to refer to her as wild: for example, Mitch accuses her of lapping up Stanley's liquor "all summer like a wild cat!" (115); Stanley compares her to a tiger: "Tiger—tiger! Drop the bottle top! Drop it!" (130). The reason for calling Blanche the wild card is her extraordinary versatility when it comes to role-playing.

Elia Kazan suggests that in the eleven scenes of the play, Blanche plays eleven different people. "And all these 11 self-dramatized and romantic chracters should be out of the romantic tradition of the pre-Bellum South, etc. Example: Sc. 2 Gay Miss Devil-may-care."[52] In fact, Blanche can be seen as playing several roles even within the same scene.

In scene 2, before any card playing has taken place, Blanche and Stanley talk cards:

> *Blanche.* You're simple, straightforward and honest, a little bit on the primitive side I should think. To interest you a woman would have to— [*She pauses with an indefinite gesture.*]
> *Stanley* [*slowly*]. Lay . . . her cards on the table.
>   . . . .

Blanche. All right; now Mr. Kowalski, let us proceed without any more double-talk. I'm ready to answer all questions. I've nothing to hide. (SND, 39–40)

Blanche and Stanley's dialogue is saturated with the language of card playing. A few moments later, the overarching card playing metaphors continue:

Stanley. If I didn't know that you was my wife's sister I'd get ideas about you!
Blanche. Such as what!
Stanley. Don't play so dumb. You know what!
Blanche [*she puts the atomizer on the table*]. All right. Cards on the table. That suits me. [*She turns to Stanley.*] I know I fib a good deal. After all a woman's charm is fifty per cent illusion, but when a thing is important I tell the truth, and this is the truth: I haven't cheated on my sister or you or anyone else as long as I have lived.

(SND, 41)

The best metaphor for the absence of dissimulation that Stanley can come up with is "cards on the table," but the question is—is such a position possible? Can either character or any character reveal a "real" self outside of dissimulation? This, incidentally, is the problem facing any biographer—the difficulty of finding that illusory "real" person— as we saw in chapter 1. Indeed, how can any biographer or aspiring biographer find it when subjects themselves may be unsure who they are? Williams, for instance, claimed that he knew his characters better than he knew himself.[53] This may be because character is more knowable in so far as it is a function of writing.

Blanche's "I've nothing to hide" suggests that she is above dissimulation, but immediately after apparently agreeing to "cards on the table," by saying "That suits me," she admits that she "fibs a good deal." Notice how even here her word choices can be seen in the context of poker playing: "suits" may remind us of the suits in a pack of cards; a "deal" is of course what initiates each hand, and we may think of "a good deal" as one that seems to present us with a strong hand.

In scene 1 she prefaces her description to Stella concerning the demise of Belle Reve by saying "I'm not meaning this in any reproachful way" (25), but she clearly reproaches Stella, "But you are the one that abandoned Belle Reve, not I! I stayed and fought for it, bled for it, almost died for it!" (26). Thus she is somewhat disingenuous, for even as she denies being reproachful, she reproaches her sister. In scene 2, Blanche's comment on Stanley's "impressive judicial air" suggests that he is putting on airs, performing; and of course, Stanley's comment on Blanche's playing "dumb" suggests that she too is performing. These conversations at the beginning of the play, then, may be read as a continuation of or prelude to the poker game, and a parallel is established between acting and poker playing. In scene 3, Blanche lies to Mitch when she claims that she is younger than Stella, and in the same scene, she fibs about her drinking habits: "I'm not accustomed to having more than one drink" (55). As the play progresses, the characters become more and more aware of Blanche's pervasive lying although Stanley claims that he has always been able to see through Blanche's lies: "I've been on to you from the start! Not once did you pull any wool over this boy's eyes!" (127) Although she has admitted to fibbing, Blanche will not admit to lying:

> *Mitch.* You lied to me, Blanche.
> *Blanche.* Don't say I lied to you . . .
> *Mitch.* Lies, lies, inside and out, all lies.
> *Blanche.* Never inside, I didn't lie in my heart.

> (119)

Mitch's inside/outside distinction appears to offer Blanche a way out. Blanche, a quintessential romantic, presents the heart as the location for truth. For Blanche, this is the position outside lies and tricks?[54] But what does it mean, "I didn't lie in my heart"? Is Blanche suggesting that there is one place where lies cannot penetrate? Could this be a position outside of role-playing? A place where a person is actually him or herself? Just as there is lying, according to Mitch, inside and out, there is role-playing inside and out: in the poker game and in the play that surrounds the poker game.

Although at one point Mitch says to Blanche, "I like you to be exactly the way that you are" (87), does he really know who she is? Does anybody know who she is? How can she be restricted to a single role? Is there one role within which she plays the other roles? In poker a player may let the wild card function as itself, in other words, at its face value, but in theater how can the character function as himself or herself? How can a character have any role outside of role-playing?

In scene 6 Blanche attempts to play La Dame au Camellias and tries to get Mitch to play Armand. In the following scene, when Stanley tries to explain Blanche's past to Stella, his language reflects his awareness of Blanche's play acting:

The trouble with Dame Blanche is that she couldn't put on her act any more in Laurel! They got wised up after two or three dates with her and then they quit, and she goes on to another, the same old act, same old hooey! . . . That's why she's here this summer, visiting royalty, putting on all this act.

(SND, 100)

During this account, Blanche is singing about "a paper moon": "It wouldn't be make-believe / If you believed in me!"—drawing even more attention to her role as an actress. Stanley's various names for her indicate some of her roles: "Dame Blanche," "Sister Blanche," "Hoity-Toity," and so on. Her incessant role-playing is reflected in her constant need for costume changes; of course, "clothes are [her] pas-sion!" (SND, 38). Throughout the play she spends her time dressing and undressing, and she constantly draws attention to these changes. In scene 10 she puts on "a white satin evening gown and a pair of scuffed silver slippers." She is like an actress playing a fairy-tale prin-cess, waiting in her dressing room, "before the mirror of the dressing table." She is "murmuring excitedly as if to a group of spectral admir-ers" (122), and by extension, the theater audience. In the scene that follows, inventing a tale about a millionaire from Dallas and a miracu-lous telegram, she has to improvise "feverishly" (120). The audience, like Stanley, quickly senses that nothing she says can be taken at its face value. "And look at yourself!" says Stanley. "Take a look at your-self in that worn out Mardi Gras outfit, rented for fifteen cents from some rag-picker! And with that crazy crown on! What queen do you think you are?" (127). The wild card is taking on the value of queen.

In an issue of *Theater* dedicated to examining the theatricality of events outside what we normally think of as theater, Daniel Gerould examines the way that actors have portrayed and continue to portray illnesses at medical conferences. In "Imaginary Invalids: A Theater of Simulated Patients," he recalls the work of Dr. Jean-Martin Charcot who worked extensively with hysterical patients at the Salpêtrière asylum in Paris and discovered the intensity of the play-acting element in hysteria. Emphasizing "the histrionic appeal of hysteria," Gerould refers to a play by André de Lorde, *A Lesson at the Salpêtrière,* which makes the use of André Pierre Brouillet's celebrated painting "A Clinical Lesson of Dr. Charcot at the Salpêtrière" [showing a demon-stration with the star performer, Blanche Wittmann 'Queen of the Hysterics'] for its setting, title, and atmosphere.[55] Curiously, Wil-liams's star performer is also called "Blanche," and her incessant role-

playing quite possibly symptomatic of hysteria. In Charcot's experiments with female patients, as Gerould points out, "it would have
been difficult to distinguish true illness signs from those that were
feigned."[56] Charcot's experiments indicate then that the line between
hysteria and role-playing is difficult to draw. One might indeed ask
whether people either on-stage or off-stage ever play themselves? Is
there a self outside of role-playing? It is easy to speculate that with
role-playing the individual pretends to be someone other than his or
her real self, but how can we know who or what this "real" self is?
What if, as Bruce Wilshire maintains, "the self that appears behind
the various social roles it performs is itself another performance" and
"there is no essential or atomic self behind the appearances"?[57] Blanche
DuBois sings, "Say it's only a paper moon, Sailing over a cardboard
sea/—But it wouldn't be make-believe If you believed in me" (SND,
99). But how can we envisage a "real" Blanche DuBois, a Blanche
DuBois outside of her role-playing? Similarly, and I return inevitably
to the Blanche–Williams parallel, how can we envisage a "real" Tennessee Williams outside of his role-playing?

Williams has frequently confessed to being a ham at heart, and his
own predilection for lying and role-playing is well known.[58] Not only
did Williams need to create theater in his writing, but he needed his
life and the life of people around him to be as theatrical as possible.
Incessant histrionics seemed to be part of Williams's family history.
Spoto points out that Williams's mother performed in amateur theater,
and "her greatest performance was perhaps that of the archetypal
'Southern Belle,' a role that Ohio-born Edwina played so well that it
finally became her life" (KS, 6).

Dotson Rader compares Williams's lifestyle to that of his father:
"Like his father, he spent much of his life in hotels, living out of
suitcases and dining on room service, liked booze and wild parties,
opened up his life to street boys and hustlers with whom he had
fleeting affairs. He could not settle down; he required drama, self-
drama, a continuous commotion and social disturbance" (TCH,
227).

Earlier in the book, Rader gives an extremely vivid account of an
occasion in Key West when Williams was desperately in need of
drugs and tried to get some from a doctor. This is another example of
Williams's role-playing. The doctor is to visit the house at 11:00 P.M.
Rader has to "act suitably frightened by Tennessee's condition, the
fragility of his health; in short, to create a deep sense of doom about

his present state," and "Tennessee would do his best to enact the death scene from Camille" (TCH, 58). The scheme appears to be working until the doctor, himself an addict/pusher, refuses to accept a check. "It's midnight. Where the hell can I cash a check at *midnight*," raves Tennessee. "This is not a frivolous matter, doctor. It is life or death! I'm at death's door!" At that moment, "Tennessee promptly toppled to the floor, right on cue, completing the last act of *Camille*." Rader suggests that "Tennessee played dead better than anybody," but Radar also did some acting of his own, running to the phone, saying that he would call the police. Then the Williams–Rader performance pays off as the doctor let them have the pills and "quickly agreed to pick up the cash the next day" (TCH, 59).

Williams's own role-playing then provides innumerable problems for the would-be biographer or any one interested in trying to bring together his life and his works. As Donald Windham, whose relationship with Williams seems to have been particularly intense, points out, Tennessee Williams's biographers have chosen a notoriously difficult subject:

> I felt that without an emotional necessity to understand, which demanded the facing of all the contradictions and confusions, there was little chance that these biographers would understand the complexity of the task they had undertaken or of the enigma they had set out to put down in words.[59]

Even people who spent a great deal of time with Williams, even those who had intimate relationships with him may not have been able to see the "real" Williams. Even if one writes out of what Windham calls "emotional necessity," and here Windham hints at his own emotional dependence on the Williams he knew, Williams is notoriously difficult to pin down. Windham goes on to suggest that "he [i.e., Tennessee Williams] assumed surrogate personalities, surrogate biographies, trying them on like suits of other peoples' clothes and substituting them for his own when they fitted the part he was playing, sometimes briefly, sometimes more or less permanently."[60] Windham entitles his essay, "AS IF: A Personal View of Tennessee Williams," and argues that Williams "feigned an emotional connection to people. For him, it was always *as if*."[61] In *Tennessee: Cry of the Heart*, Rader includes a picture of Williams in his Key West home. "He is wearing his gold Chinese 'imperial' robe, and a woman's wig. It is late," says Rader, "and we are drunk, and are about to make the rounds of the bars in Key West with Tennessee playing the role of his sister Rose, and me playing Tennessee" (TCH, 231). Williams's sister Rose had undergone a lobotomy in the 1930s, something that left her incapable of looking after herself and left her, according to Rader, with a mental age of about six. Williams to some extent blamed himself for not intervening to prevent the horrendous lobotomy although he was away at college at the time and the decision to go ahead with the terrible operation was really his mother's. There had always been a special bond between brother and sister, and this would continue until the end of the play-wright's life. In later years, in order to humor Rose, who thought that she was the "real" queen of England (the one in Buckingham palace being an imposter), Tennessee would make little bows before her. (TCH, 14) Maria St. Just explains that following the playwright's death, she went to visit Rose to break the news. "I saw on her dressing table a postcard written from Rome, which was Tennessee's last communication to her. It said, 'Dear Rose, I will be seeing you soon. Love, Rose.'"[62]

Williams' the creator of so many names, is here taking on another name. His own name, Tennessee, of course, is not his original name. There are diverse and conflicting accounts of how he got the name Tennessee, all part of the Williams mystique. In *Memoirs* the play-wright explains it in terms of family descent. His father, for example, was directly descended from John Williams, the first senator from the state of Tennessee. Elsewhere Williams maintains that he acquired the name Tennessee at the University of Iowa. "The fellows in my class," says Williams, "could only remember that I was from a South-ern state with a long name. And when they couldn't think of Missis-sippi, they settled on Tennessee. That was all right with me, so when it stuck I changed it permanently" (CN, 4). "The two states from which Tennessee Williams actually came," as Bruce Smith points out, "Were Mississippi and Missouri, hardly candidates for given names of theatrical resonance."[63] I don't buy Williams own story about his class-mates—fascinated by names, Williams invented his own name and made it into the name by which the world would know him. Donald Windham claims that Williams "helped to create legends and created them himself—as he had from the days when he made up the name Tennessee."[64]

Williams, then, was not adverse to using different names. I am sure he had no objection to film director Visconti calling him Blanche during the Roman production of *A Streetcar Named Desire*.[65] Then, in one of his last notes he signs himself Rose, completely identifying with another. Although the author of the note (Tennessee) and the reader (Rose) may be seen here as merging, as becoming one, the signature still requires a counter signature. Rose may wonder why her brother signs with her name. Is it inadvertent or is it in keeping with a secret code of which only brother and sister are aware? Is it part of an act, a game?

In his life outside his writing and within the writing itself, whether in the form of plays, short stories, novels, poems, letters, or even postcards, Williams may be seen as an inveterate game player. In his life, the only constant is the writing or to be more precise, the act of writing itself which seems indefatigable. Having once begun the game of writing, Williams cannot stop. "I never can remember a time when I wasn't restless," says Williams. "Even when I was a child I never wanted to finish a game" (CN, 104). With writing, however, Williams is caught up in a game or play that he cannot control.

In his preface to *Collected Stories*, Williams gives a more extensive account of the all-consuming nature of his work: "After my morning's work, I have little to give but indifference to people. I try to excuse myself with the pretense that my work justifies this lack of caring much for almost anything else. Sometimes I crack through the emotional block. I touch, I embrace, I hold tight to a necessary companion. But the breakthrough is not long lasting. Morning returns, and only work matters again" (CS, xv). Elsewhere he writes in poor French, *"il n'y a rien que le travail!"*[66]—there is nothing but work. How similar this is to Derrida's "I refer to myself, this is writing, I am writing, this is writing" (SS, 54). It is as if there is, indeed, nothing outside of writing. The play of the writing is indeed "no longer the play of someone who plays" (EO, 69). In order to think of play in a radical sense," says Derrida, "perhaps one must think beyond the activity of a subject manipulating objects according to or against rules, et cetera" (EO, 69). Rather than manipulating, then, Williams himself is being manipulated by his own writing. Tennessee Williams, as self, as biographical subject can only be an effect of the work of writing itself.

In another letter to Maria St. Just written from the Hotel Élyssée in 1973, Williams is in a despondent mood following the unsuccessful run of his play *Out Cry*. "I feel like my writing career is washed up. I go on writing but it means nothing to me," says Williams, "The revivals of *Streetcar* received lavish praise but it's no real comfort as my only real joy in writing is continuing with it."[67] Like the play acting, the writing will go on right up until Williams's death that, of

course, is also somewhat theatrical; but even after the death the writing will continue through the counter-signature, that is to say, through
readers differing reappropriations of Williams's texts. "It is the ear
of the other than signs," says Derrida. "Every text answers to this
structure. . . . A text is signed only much later by the other" (EO, 51).

Toward the end of his life, Williams continued to play poker. In
1967, he writes to Maria St. Just:

> Life is pretty dull except for the poker nights twice a week. I have become
> quite good at poker because of my fishy eyes which betray no emotion
> whether I have a royal flush or nothing in my hand. Last night I was the
> big winner, over forty bucks in coin of the realm.
> How sad it is to have nothing else to tell you!
>
> Much love, 10[69]

For Williams writing usually means the writing of plays. Through
the act of playwriting/poker playing Williams, often described as a
shy man, is forced into playing roles, is forced into taking to the stage:
the staging of his signature.

The emblem for Williams writing may be the poker playing. The
qualities of poker, as we have seen, figure those of plays. Poker, however, is a dangerous game. One may risk losing all that one has. One
may want to play on, to never stop playing—always wanting new
hands, different cards. There will, however, always be one more
hand—if not tonight, tomorrow will do, but the last hand can never
be played and the game will go on after the initial player or players
leave the game.

Nevertheless through the act of writing, Williams enters the game,
a game that is not merely "play for the sake of play," but that is a
game which all who read or see his plays may also enter, and in so
doing, enable the playwright to live on, to survive. For the writer to
live on, he or she requires an active reader who like the writer is
prepared to run the risk of entering the game. "If you bet nothing,
you win nothing," says David Wood, "He who dares wins."[69]

Because it depends on the action of the reader, the signature is
always deferred. The third modality of the signature "inscribes itself as
act (action and archive)" (S/S, 54). Even if, and this seems extremely
unlikely, Williams plays do not continue to be staged, there is of
course the "archive" the public place where writing will always be,
where Tennessee Williams will always be monumentalized.

Since the pioneer work on game theory carried out by Johann Huizinga, it has been customary to distinguish between games as rule-bound and play as more spontaneous, enjoying a much greater freedom. Neither author nor biographer can ever master the game; however, for the author's texts can break the rules of the game, transcending the restrictions necessitated by game playing. Although often dead, the author is still involved in the game for with Derrida's third modality of the signature, the "I am writing, this is writing . . . excludes *nothing*" (Derrida's emphasis; S/S, 54), and this "nothing" can include the author. Contrary to the claims of those hostile to deconstruction, the author is not excluded. Through play, particularly in terms of the work of writing that involves the play of structure (the third modality of the signature, which Derrida calls "the signature of signatures") and in terms of the play of a stylistic signature (the second modality of the signature) something (a piece? a trace? a biographeme?) of the author may enter our own lives.

Conclusion

Biographical theory, of which we have as yet seen very little, as compared to say, literary theory, has begun to doubt the notion of a neat, knowable, centered self. The movement within biographical theory to advocate a more open-ended form of biography, a form of biography that does not invoke the author to cut off meaning in accordance with what he or she may or may not have intended, is very much in keeping with the movement (if we can call it that) of deconstruction. Literary biography, then, should not be afraid of deconstruction, but can turn to deconstruction to examine and even enrich itself.

Here I have attempted to imagine and describe a form of postmodern biography that draws on some of the thinking of Roland Barthes and Jacques Derrida. I have suggested that this project has three fundamental needs.

First, there is a need to recognize that the biographical subject is dispersed and that, therefore, we should be particularly sensitive to intertextuality—to relations between an author's texts, those texts' pre-texts, and texts (written by others) that claim that they deal with the author's life.

Second, we need to recognize the importance of the proper name, which is also included in the intertextual network. This may be the name of the author, but it may also—as in the case of Tennessee Williams—be the name of one of the author's characters. Indeed, it is possible to think of an author's texts as being generated out of a proper name. Blanche DuBois's name is expressed across the whole of Williams's corpus. Her name founds a space of writing in which Tennessee Williams himself can be seen as living in a country of the blue, where he laments to the melancholy sound of the blues musicians who play their wooden instruments (made of wood, *du bois*) in many a bar where Williams pursues the beautiful boy.

Third, postmodern biography needs to consider signature effects and to take seriously Derrida's suggestions concerning the signature's different modalities. The second modality, in keeping with postmodernism's privileging of surface rather than depth, involves the writer's style and resists the leap to the thematic. The rigorous examination of the text's surface reveals repetitive marks, which even if they constitute an opposition (as they do in the case of Tennessee Williams) may still be regarded as a stylistic signature. By drawing attention to the "act" of production, the third modality invokes the work of writing itself. As long as people continue to encounter the author's texts, production is ongoing. Although the author's signature depends on the counter-signature, the signature of "the other," neither author nor reader can have the last word.

It should be clear by now that connecting author and text is a far more intricate process than is generally thought. The kind of biography that I have in mind urges us to pay attention not to filiation but to connection. Connection enables us to imagine that a corpus is generated out of a proper name. Connection enables us to imagine that a work is not engendered by a life (the life of a writer) but by the border between life and work. "Neither 'immanent' readings of philosophical systems . . . nor external, empirical genetic-readings," says Derrida, "have ever in themselves questioned the *dynamis* of that borderline between the 'work' and the 'life,' the system and the subject of the system" (Derrida's emphasis, EO 5).

Having come across Barthes's essay or perhaps just the title of it, "The Death of the Author," many people seem to assume that postmodern thinkers have no interest in the biographical subject. This, however, I believe I have shown is far from the case. The "author" is a vitally important "subject" for both Barthes and Derrida. As cited at the beginning of this study, Derrida says, "The subject is absolutely indispensable. I don't destroy the subject; I situate it." He admits, "one cannot get along without the notion of subject. It is a question of knowing where it comes from and how it functions."[1]

Derrida's work has often been criticized for its intimidating obscurity, and it may be the last place where most people working on the theory of literary biography would look for enlightenment. These people may also have heard that Derrida reduces the self to an effect of language; and wanting to retain the romantic notion of a flesh and blood author, they again feel that they must shun deconstruction. My response to them here is that although Derrida may indeed maintain that the subject is an effect of language, he would not for a minute, agree that the self is therefore reducible to the linguistic; for the "dynamis" that he emphasizes borders both the work and the life.

Finally, I should make it clear that my observations and suggestions concerning the theory of biography are not intended to undermine the work of traditional biographers. I am addressing those who theorize about biography and not necessarily those engaged in writing biographies. As with deconstruction itself, however, with the kind of biography that I have in mind, theory and practice are really inseparable.

Abbreviations

This list contains abbreviations used for Tennessee Williams's works only. Abbreviations for other frequently cited works, particularly works by Barthes and Derrida, are given in the notes.

AB   *American Blues: Five Short Plays*
BA   *Battle of Angels*
CT   *Cat on a Hot Tin Roof*
CR   *Camino Real*
CS   *Collected Stories*
GM   *The Glass Menagerie*
IWC   *In The Winter of Cities: Poems*
MS   *Memoirs*
MW   *Moise and the World of Reason*
NI   *The Night of the Iguana*
OD   *Orpheus Descending*
SBY   *Sweet Bird of Youth*
SLS   *Suddenly Last Summer*
SND   *A Streetcar Named Desire*
SS   *Summer and Smoke*
27W   *27 Wagons Full of Cotton and Other One Act Plays*
WL   *Where I Live: Selected Essays*

Notes

Preface

    1. Dotson Rader, *Tennessee: Cry of the Heart* (New York: Doubleday, 1985), p. 124. Abbreviated TCH in parenthetical page references within the text.
    2. Roland Barthes, *S/Z*, trans. Richard Miller (New York: Hill and Wang, 1974), p. 211. Barthes' emphasis.
    3. See Roland Barthes, *Image-Music-Text*, trans. Stephen Heath (New York: Hill and Wang, 1975), p. 161. Abbreviated IMT.
    4. William Gass, "Mr. Blockner, Mr. Feaster, and Mr. Faulkner," *New York Review of Books* (27 June 1974): 4.
    5. Norman K. Denzin, *Interpretive Biography* (Newberry Parks, Calif.: Sage Publications, 1989), p. 25.
    6. Roland Barthes, "Theory of the Text," in *Untying the Text: A Poststructuralist Reader*, ed. Robert Young (Boston: Routledge and Kegan Paul, 1981), p. 39. Abbreviated TT.

Chapter 1. Literary Biography's Quest for the Biographical Subject

    1. Leon Edel, *Literary Biography* (Toronto: Toronto University Press, 1957; Bloomington: Indiana University Press, 1973), p. 2.
    2. Richard Altick, *Lives and Letters: A History of Literature and Biography in England and America* (New York: Alfred A. Knopf, 1965), p. xi.
    3. Lee and Gosse's views are among many others adumbrated in the most comprehensive survey of biographical theory that I have come across, David Novarr's *The Lines of Life: Theories of Biography, 1880–1990* (West Lafayette, Ind.: Purdue University Press, 1986). The quotes from Lee and Gosse are on p. 12 and p. 16.
    4. Ibid., p. 50.
    5. In fact, both Gosse and Nicholson do rely on science because both are concerned about psychology. Gosse may have been the first to introduce the term into the discussion of biography—psychology was a term not mentioned by Lee (ibid., p. 16). Novarr makes it clear that although Nicholson often talked about the "art" of biography, he had a strong belief in science, and especially psychology (ibid., p. 47).
    6. Quoted in ibid., p. 53.
    7. Ibid.
    8. Ibid., p. 54.
    9. For Ellman's view see Dennis W. Petrie, *Ultimately Fiction: Design in Modern American Literary Biography* (West Lafayette, Ind.: Purdue University Press, 1981), p. 41.
    10. Petrie borrows the phrase "ultimately fiction" from Malamud and uses it in his title, *Ultimately Fiction: Design in Modern American Literary Biography*. I take

Petrie's thesis to be that literary biography should "aspire to the condition of fiction in its aesthetic design" (p. 58).

11. Bernard Malamud, *Dubin's Lives* (New York: Farrar, Straus and Giroux, 1979), p. 98.

12. Paul Murray Kendall, *The Art of Biography* (New York: Norton, 1965; Toronto: George J. McLeod; London: George Allen and Unwin), pp. x–xi.

13. Ibid., pp. 13–14.

14. Justin Kaplan, "The 'Real Life,'" in *Studies in Biography*, ed. Daniel Aaron (Cambridge: Harvard University Press, 1978), p. 2.

15. *Dubin's Lives*, pp. 303–4.

16. *Literary Biography*, p. 43. In a similar vein Richard Altick claimed for literary biography an ability to open "the windows of the soul" (*Lives and Letters*, p. xi).

17. In her book on Virginia Woolf, Phyllis Rose also links biography to mythology, arguing that when we write our own lives we create "a personal mythology." She sees "biographical criticism" as "moving toward the recognition that a life is as much a work of fiction—of guiding narrative structures—as novels and poems, and that the task of literary biography is to explore this fiction" (*Woman of Letters: A Life of Virginia Woolf* [New York: Oxford University Press, 1978], p. viii).

18. Leon Edel, "The Figure Under the Carpet," in *Telling Lives: The Biographer's Art*, ed. Marc Pachter (Washington, D. C.: New Republic, 1979), p. 25.

19. Ibid., p. 18.

20. *Writing Lives: principia biographica* (New York: Norton, 1984), p. 145.

21. Quoted in *The Lines of Life*, p. 43.

22. *Lives and Letters*, pp. 402, 411. Leslie Fielder is quoted on p. 402.

23. See, for example, "The Figure Under the Carpet," p. 21.

24. *Ultimately Fiction*, p. 18.

25. Ibid., p. 74.

26. Leon Edel, "Biography and the Science of Man," in *New Directions in Biography*, ed. Antony M. Friedson (Manoa: Univ. of Hawaii Press, 1981), pp. 7–8.

27. Ibid., p. 3.

28. Quoted in Petrie, *Ultimately Fiction* p. 18.

29. See especially *Writing Lives*, pp. 140, 131, 27; and *Literary Biography*, p. 53.

30. Albert J. Devlin, ed., *Conversations with Tennessee Williams*, (Jackson: University Press of Mississippi, 1986), p. 108. Abbreviated CN.

31. Tennessee Williams, Introduction to *The Dark at the Top of the Stairs*, by William Inge (New York: Random House, 1958), p. vii.

32. Williams, "Man Named Tennessee," *Newsweek* (1 April 1957): 81.

33. Signi L. Falk, *Tennessee Williams* (Boston: Twayne/G. K. Hall, 1978). See especially pp. 21–22.

34. Francis Donahue, *The Dramatic World of Tennessee Williams* (New York: Ungar, 1964), p. 218.

35. Nancy M. Tischler, *Tennessee Williams: Rebellious Puritan* (New York: Citadel Press, 1961), p. 143. For other speculations about Williams's attitude toward sex and the repurcussions for his work, see W. David Sievers, *Freud on Broadway* (New York: Hermitage House, 1955), pp. 370–88.

36. Ester M. Jackson, *The Broken World of Tennessee Williams* (Madison: University of Wisconsin Press, 1966), p. 27.

37. Arthur Ganz, "The Desperate Morality of the Plays of Tennessee Williams," in *Tennessee Williams: A Collection of Critical Essays*, ed. Stephen S. Stanton (Englewood Cliffs, N.J.: Prentice Hall, 1977), pp. 123–37; Edwina Dakin Williams and Shepherd Mead, *Remember Me to Tom* (New York: Putnam, 1983), pp. 13–14. For discussion of morality in Williams's work see also Paul J. Hurley, "Tennessee Wil-

liams: the Playwright as Social Critic," *The Theater Annual* 21 (1964): 40–56 and Ingrid Rogers, *Tennessee Williams: A Moralist's Answer to the Problems of Life* (Frankfurt: Peter Lang Frankfurt/M. Herbert Lang Bern, 1976).

38. See Mike Steen, *A Look at Tennessee Williams* (New York: Hawthorne Books, 1969), pp. 205–56.

39. George-Michel Sarotte, *Like a Brother, Like a Lover: Male Homosexuality in the American Novel and Theatre from Herman Melville to James Baldwin,* trans. Richard Miller (Garden City, N.Y.: Anchor Press/ Doubleday, 1978), p. 107; Dervin, "The Spook in the Rainforest: The Incestuous Structure of Tennessee Williams's Plays," *Psychocultural Review* 3 (Summer–Fall, 1979): 158–83.

40. Foster Hirsch, *A Portrait of the Artist: The Plays of Tennessee Williams* (Port Washington, N.Y.: Kennikat Press, 1979). Quotations are on pp. 5, 10, 12, 14, 15, 17.

41. C. W. E. Bigsby, *A Critical Introduction to Twentieth Century Drama 2: Tennessee Williams Arthur Miller Edward Albee* (Cambridge: Cambridge University Press, 1984), p. 6.

42. Ibid., p. 20.

43. Ibid., p. 5.

44. Ibid., p. 20.

45. Ibid., pp. 78–79.

46. Quoted in Ethan Mordden, *The American Theater* (New York: Oxford University Press, 1981), p. 245.

47. Donald Spoto, *The Kindness of Strangers: The Life of Tennessee Williams* (Boston: Little, Brown and Co., 1985), p. 186. Abbreviated KS.

48. Ibid., p. 187.

49. See Steen, *A Look at Tennessee Williams,* p. 267.

50. Bigsby, *A Critical Introduction,* p. 80.

51. Ibid.

52. Williams's comment about "the more accustomed implausibility of the street" reminds me of Irma's suggestion to the audience at the end of Genet's *The Balcony:* "You must go home, where everything—you can be sure—will be falser than here." (Jean Genet, *The Balcony,* trans. Bernard Frechtman [New York: Grove Press, 1958], p. 96).

53. The quote is from Hirsch, *A Portrait of the Artist,* p. 17.

54. The quote is from Kaplan, "'The Real Life,'" in Aaron, *Studies in Biography,* p. 2.

55. *Writing Lives,* p. 14.

Chapter 2. Literary Biography Turns to Intertextuality and the Proper Name

1. James Clifford, "Hanging Up Looking Glasses at Odd Corners: Ethnobiographical Perspectives," in *Studies in Biography,* ed. Aaron, p. 44.

2. Ibid., p. 45.

3. Ibid., p. 56.

4. Ibid., p. 45. The Camus' quotation is from *Carnets, 1942–51,* Vol. 2, trans. P. Thody (London: Hamilton, 1966), p. 17.

5. Roland Barthes, *Criticism and Truth,* trans. Katrine Pilcher Keuneman (London: The Athlone Press, 1987), pp. 75–76. Abbreviated CT.

6. Eric Homberger and John Charmley, *The Troubled Face of Biography* (Basingstoke: Macmillan, 1988), p. x.

7. Susan Sontag, "Writing Itself: On Roland Barthes," in *Barthes: Selected Writings,* ed. Susan Sontag (New York: Hill and Wang), p. xx.

8. Ibid., p. xxxiii.

9. Ibid.

10. Ibid., n. 2.

11. Roland Barthes, *Sade/Fourier/Loyola* (New York: Hill and Wang, 1976), p. 8. Abbreviated SFL.

12. Textual analysis is comparable both to "the science of literature" sketched in *Criticism and Truth* and to "poetics" that concerns itself with the rules or conventions which make meaninging possible rather than with meaning itself. For Barthes' understanding of the term "poetics," see also "The Structuralist Activity," in Barthes, *Critical Essays,* trans. Richard Howard (Evanston, Ill.: Northwestern University Press, 1972), p. 218.

13. Michael Holroyd, "How I Fell into Biography," in Homberger and Charmley, *The Troubled Face of Biography,* p. 102.

14. Malcolm Bradbury, "The Telling Life: Some Thoughts on Literary Biography," in *The Troubled Face of Biography,* p. 135.

15. As I pointed out earlier, Barthes also distinguishes the work from the text by suggesting that "the work is a finished object, something computable, which can occupy a physical space. . . . The work is held in the hand, the text in language" (TT, 39).

16. Quoted in Paul L. Jay, "Being in the Text: Autobiography and the Problem of the Subject" *MLN* 97.4 (December 1982): 1046.

17. Ibid., p. 1052.

18. Ibid., p. 1058.

19. My translation; Julia Kristeva, *Séméiotiké: Recherches pour une sémanalyse* (Paris: Editions de Seuil, 1969), p. 146. See also Kristeva, *Desire in Language: A Semiotic Approach to Literature and Art,* ed. Leon S. Roudiez, trans. Thomas Gora, Alice Jardine, and Leon S. Roudiez (New York: Columbia University Press, 1980), especially chap. 3, "Word, Dialogue, and Novel."

20. J. P. Plottel and H. Charney, *Intertextuality: New Perspectives in Criticism* (New York: New York Literary Forum, 1978), p. xix.

21. Roland Barthes, *Roland Barthes by Roland Barthes,* trans. Richard Howard (New York: Hill and Wang, 1977), p. 172.

22. Barthes' emphasis. Roland Barthes, *S/Z,* trans. Richard Miller (New York: Hill and Wang, 1974), p. 211.

23. Harold Bloom, *The Anxiety of Influence: A Theory of Poetry* (New York: Oxford University Press, 1973), p. 15.

24. Jacques Derrida, *Positions,* trans. Alan Bass (Chicago: University of Chicago Press, 1981), p. 36; and *Writing and Difference,* trans. Alan Bass (Chicago: University of Chicago Press, 1981), pp. 142–43.

25. G. B. Madison, *The Hermeneutics of Postmodernity: Figures and Themes* (Bloomington and Indianapolis: Indiana University Press, 1988), p. 111.

26. Jacques Derrida, *Of Grammatology,* trans. Gyatri Chakravorty Spivak (Baltimore: Johns Hopkins University Press, 1976), p. 158. Abbreviated OG.

27. *The Hermeneutics of Postmodernity,* p. 111.

28. E. Warwick Slinn,"Deconstruction and Meaning: The Textuality Game," *Philosophy and Literature* 12.1 (April 1988): 82.

29. Jacques Derrida, *Dissemination,* trans. Barbara Johnson (Chicago: University of Chicago Press, 1981), p. 219. Abbreviated DS.

30. The word "allusion" is of course from the Latin *ludere* to play; hence the ludic quality of allusion.

31. Jacques Derrida, *Signéponge/Signsponge,* trans. Richard Rand (New York: Columbia University Press, 1984), p. 22 Abbreviated S/S.

32. This is J. S. Mill's position as stated in *A System of Logic.* See John Searle, *Speech Acts: An Essay in the Philosophy of Language* (London: Cambridge University Press, 1969), p. 163.

33. Ibid., p. 170.

34. Ibid., p. 169.

35. Ibid., p. 172.

36. Christopher Norris, *Deconstruction and the Interests of Theory* (London: Printer Publishers, 1988), p. 230.

37. Bradbury, "The Telling Life," in *The Troubled Face of Biography,* p. 134.

38. Jacques Derrida, *The Ear of the Other: Otobiography, Transference, Translation,* trans. Peggy Kamuf (Lincoln: University of Nebraska Press, 1985), p. 72. Abbreviated EO. Perhaps the most well known of Derrida's own (auto)biographical readings is his reading of Freud in "Coming Into One's Own," in *Psychoanalysis and the Question of the Text: Selected Papers from the English Institute, 1976–77,* ed. Geoffrey Hartman (Baltimore: Johns Hopkins University Press, 1978), pp. 114–148. See Paul Jay, "What's the Use? Critical Theory and the Study of Autobiography," *Biography* 10, no. 1 (Winter 1987): 42.

39. Rainer Maria Rilke, *Duino Elegies and Sonnets to Orpheus,* trans. A. Poulin Jr. (Boston: Houghton Mifflin, 1977), p. 85.

40. Williams never stopped working on this play. He also rewrote it for the screen. The title of the movie was *The Fugitive Kind.* Directed by Sidney Lumet, it appeared in 1960.

41. Virgil, *The Georgics and Eclogues of Virgil,* trans. T. C. Williams (Cambridge: Harvard University Press, 1915), p. 119. Abbreviated GEV.

42. Ovid, *Metamorphoses,* ed. E. J. Kenny, trans. A. D. Melville (Oxford and New York: Oxford University Press, 1986), p. 227. Abbreviated MET.

43. We should note that in some versions of the myth, including Euripides's version, Orpheus succeeds in bringing his beloved back from Hades. See, for example, Peter Dronke, "The Return of Eurydice," *Classica et Mediaevalia* 23 (1962): 201–203.

44. John Ditsky, *The Onstage Christ: Studies in the Persistence of a Theme* (Totawa, N.J.: Barnes and Noble, 1980), p. 127.

45. See Signi Falk, *Tennessee Williams,* p. 105.

46. Williams's epigraph for *Camino Real.* The translator is unnamed.

47. Roland Barthes, *The Pleasure of the Text,* trans. Richard Miller (New York: Hill and Wang, 1975), p. 36.

48. See Jerry Preston, ed., *Blues Lyric Poetry* (New York: Garland Publishing, 1983), p. 151.

49. LeRoi Jones, *Blues People: Negro Music in White America* (New York: William Morrow, 1963), p. 50.

50. The song, "Heavenly Grass," which Val begins to sing in *Orpheus Descending* (OD, 50), is written in its entirety in Williams's collection of poems entitled *In the Winter of Cities,* where it appears as one of the "Blue Mountain Ballads," with "Lonesome Man," "Cabin," and "Sugar in the Cane." The "Blue Mountain Ballads" are followed in this collection with two other blues songs, "Kitchen Door Blues," and "Gold Tooth Blues."

51. *Blues People,* p. 62.

52. Ibid., p. 91.

53. *Negro Workaday Songs* quoted in *Blues People,* p. 91. We recall that Bessie Smith was one of the names written on Val's guitar, and Val says,"The name Bessie Smith is written in the stars" (OD, 51). For a continuing preoccupation among Ameri-

can playwrights with blues legends, see Albee's *The Death of Bessie Smith* in Edward Albee, *The Sandbox. The Death of Bessie Smith (With Fam and Yam)* (New York: Signet, 1963).

54. W. S. Anderson, "The Orpheus of Virgil and Ovid: *flebile nescio quid*" in *Orpheus: The Metamorphosis of a Myth,* ed. John Warden (Toronto: The University of Toronto Press, 1982), p. 47.

55. Ibid., p. 50, n. 17.

56. Elia Kazan, "Notebook for *A Streetcar Named Desire,*" in *Directors on Directing: A Source Book for Modern Theater,* eds. Toby Cole and Helen Krick Chinoy (Indianapolis and New York: Bobbs-Merril, 1976), p. 371.

57.Notice also that in *The Divine Comedy,* Dante marks the moment of Virgil's departure with the triple repetition of his name: "But Virgil had deprived us of himself, / Virgil, the gentlest father, Virgil he / to whom I gave myself for my salvation' (*The Divine Comedy of Dante Alighieri: Purgatorio,* trans. Allen Mandelbaum [New York: Bantam, 1984], bk. xxx, pp. 49–51).

58. The inevitability of such losses is articulated by Joe in *The Long Goodbye.* He expresses his gloomy philosophy to his friend, Silva: "You're saying good-bye all the time, every minute you live." Because that's what life is, just a long, long good-bye—to one thing after another! Till you get to the last one, Silva, and that's—goodbye to yourself!" (27W, 178).

59. Paul Oliver, *Conversation with the Blues* (New York: Horizon Press, 1986), p. 170.

60. Ibid.

61. W. C. Handy, ed. *A Treasury of the Blues: Complete Words and Music of 67 Great Songs from Memphis to the Present Day with an Historical and Critical Text by Abbe Niles* (New York: Charles Boni, 1949), p. 11.

62. *Blues People,* p. 78.

63. Quoted in Oliver, *Conversation with the Blues,* p. 25.

64. The phrase is also another title. "Stella for Star" is the title of a short story that Williams wrote as a very young man, and for which he was awarded first prize in the Winifried Erwin short story contest in early 1935. See Spoto, *The Kindness of Strangers,* p. 43.

65. It is, perhaps, no coincidence that the same lack of agreement in terms of gender occurs in the name of the former DuBois family estate Belle Reve. The noun *reve* meaning "dream" should be preceded by the masculine form of the adjective, *beau.*

66. Williams makes repeated use of the verb *blanch.* See, for example, the beginning of Nono's poem in *The Night of the Iguana:*

> How calmly does the orange branch
> Observe the sky begin to blanch
> Without a cry, without a prayer,
> With no betrayal of despair.

(NI, 123)

67. *Like A Brother,* pp. 108–109.

68. Stanley Edgar Hyman, "Some Notes on the Albertine Strategy," *Hudson Review* 6 (Autumn 1953): 417–22.

69. Maria St. Just, *Five O'Clock Angel: Letters of Tennessee Williams to Maria St. Just 1948–1982* (New York: Alfred Knopf, 1990), p. 26.

70. Gene D. Phillips, *The Films of Tennessee Williams* (Philadelphia: Art Alliance Press, 1980), pp. 81–82.

71. In scene 7, Stanley laughs at the idea of Blanche as a lily. "But Sister Blanche

is no lily! Ha-ha! Some lily she is!" (99). One definition of lily is "one that resembles the lily in whiteness, fairness, purity, or fragility" [a virgin, a most unspotted—{Shak.}]" (*Webster's*).

72. Quoted in Edgar Allen Poe, *The Poems of Edgar Allen Poe*, ed. Killis Cambell (New York: Russel and Russel, 1962), p. 272.

73. Ruby Cohn, "The Garrulous Grotesques of Tennessee Williams," in *Tennessee Williams: A Collection of Critical Essays*, ed. Stephen S. Stanton (Englewood Cliffs, N.J.: Prentice-Hall, 1977), p. 46. Notice, also, that the name DuBois is occasionally pronounced Du Boy as in the name, W. E. B. Du Bois.

74. Blanche DuBois is not the only one of Williams's characters who appears in a play where language suggests that she may be read as being a boy. Such a reading is even more obvious for Maggie in *Cat on a Hot Tin Roof*. Maggie is described as having a voice that "sometimes . . . drops as low as a boy's and you have a sudden image of her playing boy's games as a child" (CT, 18). Furthermore, like Blanche Maggie calls her husband a boy: "I'll tell you what they're up to, boy of mine!" (CT, 17). Brick's body is described as "still slim and firm as a boy" (CT, 17), and following his relationship with Skipper there are question marks surrounding his sexuality.

75. Emmet Robbins, "Famous Orpheus," in *Orpheus: The Metamorphosis of a Myth*, ed. John Warden (Toronto and Buffalo: University of Toronto Press, 1982), p. 14.

76. W. K. C. Guthrie, *Orpheus and the Greek Religion: A Study of the Orphic Movement* (New York: Norton, 1966), pp. 31–32.

77. Ibid., p. 32.

78. The editor, here, E. J. Kenny, points out that the "tradition" of Orpheus's "love for tender boys" was "attested by the Alexandrian poet Phanocles." Kenny also says that "Sandys found the lines too shocking to translate" (MET, p. 432 n. 84).

79. "The Orpheus of Ovid and Virgil: *flebile nesquio quid*," in *Orpheus: The Metamorphoses of a Myth*, ed. John Warden (Toronto: The University of Toronto Press, 1982), p. 45.

80. See, for example, R. B. Parker, "The Circle Closed: A Psychological Reading of *The Glass Menagerie* and *The Two-Character Play*," *Modern Drama* 28, no. 4 (December 1985): 527, and Gilbert Debusscher, "'Minting Their Separate Wills': Tennessee Williams and Hart Crane," *Modern Drama* 26, no. 4 (1983): 472 n. 23.

81. Donald Windham, *Lost Friendships: A memoir of Truman Capote, Tennessee Williams, and Others* (New York: William Morrow, 1983), p. 176.

82. Truman Capote, "Remembering Tennessee," *Playboy* (January 1989): pp. 228, 282.

83. Quoted in KS, 139.

84. Capote, "Remembering Tennessee," p. 228.

85. Michel Foucault, *The History of Sexuality, Volume 2, The Use of Pleasure*, trans. Robert Hurley (New York: Vintage Books, 1980), p. 223.

86. Ibid., p. 200.

87. Dakin Williams and Shepherd Mead, *Tennessee Williams: An Intimate Biography* (New York: Arbor House, 1983), p. 319.

88. Foucault, *The History of Sexuality, Volume I, An Introduction*, trans. Robert Hurley (New York: Vintage Books, 1980), p. 69.

89. The link between sexuality and darkness is a familiar one. Appropriately, Foucault describes sex as "the fragment of darkness that we each carry within us: a general signification, a universal secret, an omnipresent cause, a fear that never ends" (*The History of Sexuality, Volume 1*, p. 69).

90. Williams is clearer about the facts in an interview given in 1975 where he mentions the codicil and says of Crane, "I read of his death in 1932, when he jumped

off the stern of a ship called the Esmeralda. It was twenty-four hours north of Havana" (CN, 293). Here, then, he is more precise about the location, and he specifies the name of the ship and the part of the ship from which Crane jumped.

91. Debusscher, "Minting their Separate Wills," p. 459.

92. Ibid., pp. 460–61.

93. Quoted in KS, p. 195.

94. Capote talks about Williams's "tendency toward around-the-clock sex and gin and general carousing" ("Remembering Tennessee" p. 228).

95. Donald Windham, ed., *Tennessee Williams: Letters to Donald Windham 1940–1945* (New York: Holt, Rinehart, and Winston, 1976), p. 105.

96. Robert Graves, *The Greek Myths* (London: Penguin, 1955), p. 116. See also MET, 229–230.

97. Gore Vidal, introduction, *Collected Stories*, by Tennessee Williams, p. xxi.

98. Quoted in KS, 71.

99. *Tennessee Williams' Letters to Donald Windham*, p. 105.

100. *Duino Elegies and The Sonnets to Orpheus*, p. 93.

101. See MET, book 8.

102. *Lost Friendships*, p. 167.

103. Ibid., p. 168.

104. Dotson Rader also emphasizes Williams's laugh: "Tennessee had a very loud laugh, a cracked, machinegun-like, firecracker bark that exploded often, unexpectedly, and not infrequently at the most inappropriate moments, say during the most serious scenes of a play" (TCH, 14).

105. "Remembering Tennessee," p. 282.

Chapter 3. The Effects of Signature

1. Jacques Derrida, *Margins of Philosophy*, trans. Barbara Johnson (Chicago: University of Chicago Press, 1982), p. 328. Abbreviated MR.

2. Jean Marie Todd, *Autobiographics in Freud and Derrida* (New York: Garland Publishing, 1990), p. 101.

3. See Jacques Derrida, *Glas*, trans. John P. Leavey Jr. and Richard Rand (Lincoln and London: University of Nebraska Press, 1986), p. 84 bi. Abbreviated GL. I will follow citation procedures used by Leavey in *Glassary;* that is to say page numbers are followed by an a to indicate the left column or b for the right column. An i following the a or b indicates an insert in the column.

4. Derrida himself has admitted that in *Glas* he is also working with "the disseminated name *'derrière le rideau'*" (EO, p. 76).

5. Gregory L. Ulmer, *Teletheory: Grammatology in the Age of Video* (New York: Routledge, 1989), p. 161.

6. *Autobiographics in Freud and Derrida*, p. 133.

7. Peggy Kamuf, *Signature Pieces: On the Institution of Authorship* (Ithaca: Cornell University Press, 1988), p. viii.

8. It is a striking coincidence that the "place" of the signature is also invoked in Williams's novel, *Moise and the World of Reason*. The narrator says that "when Moise [his artist friend] completes a canvas it is truly completed, even to the almost indistinguishable M that is her signature and is worked into the painting as if it were a part of it" (MW 168).

9. Kazan, "Notebook for *A Streetcar Named Desire*," p. 373.

10. Ibid., p. 374.

11. Luce Irigaray, *This Sex Which Is Not One*, trans. Carolyn Porter with Carolyn Burke (Ithaca: Cornell University Press, 1985), p. 142.

12. Foucault, *The History of Sexuality, Volume 2*, p. 145.

13. Ibid., p. 147.

14. *This Sex*, p. 25.

15. Anca Vlasopolos, "Authorizing History: Victimization in *A Streetcar Named Desire*," *Theatre Journal* (October 1986): 334.

16. *This Sex*, p. 83.

17. Ibid., p.144.

18. "Authorizing History," p. 327. An obvious example of her economic dependence on others is her drinking of Stanley's liquor, which she is accused of "lapping . . . up all summer like a wildcat!" (SND, 115).

19. *This Sex*, p. 172.

20. Ibid., p. 187.

21. Ibid., p. 188.

22. "Notebook for *A Streetcar Named Desire*," p. 373.

23. *This Sex*, p. 84.

24. Ibid., p. 25.

25. *The History of Sexuality, Volume 2*, p. 47.

26. Steen, *A Look at Tennessee Williams*, p. 201.

27. Quoted in Hirsch, *A Portrait of the Artist*, pp. 6–7.

28. See Windham, *Lost Friendships*, p. 167.

29. See St. Just, *Five O'Clock Angel*, p. 20.

30. *Lost Friendships*, p. 226.

31. "Man Named Tennessee," p. 81.

32. In "The Double Session" Derrida goes on to explore the phonic signifier *or* as distributed throughout some of Mallarmé's texts. (DS, 262–65).

33. Ortrun Zuber, "The Translation of Non-Verbal Signs in Drama," *Pacific Quarterly* 5 (1980): 66.

34. Quoted in Phillips, *The Films of Tennessee Williams*, p. 75.

35. Zuber, "The Translation," p. 69. Notice also that the connection between "stud," the *st* signifier, and Stanley can be seen in the striking number of *s* and *t*'s in Pablo's cursing of Stanley's rutting luck in the last scene; *"MaldiTa Sea Tu SuerTo!"* (SND, 131). There is the suggestion that Stanley, the stud, is not only able to have the men at cards, but also to have the women.

36. Blue is everywhere in Williams's work irrespective of the season: "These summer days are hot and blue." "These winter nights are blue and cold" ("Sugar in the Cane," IWC, 104).

37. Oliver, *Conversation with The Blues*, p. 170.

38. St. Just, *Five O'Clock Angel*, p. 193. Donald Windham points out that "his intimate name was Tenn. And if he was feeling particularly close to you he signed his letters 10" (*Lost Friendships*, p. 174).

39. I am reminded here of Williams's essay "On A Streetcar Named Success" where Williams explains the experience of suddenly becoming a celebrity. This happened to him immediately after the Chicago opening of *The Glass Menagerie*. He argues that the person in this situation "comes to know that the public somebody that you are when you 'have a name' is a fiction created with mirrors and that the only person worth being is the solitary and unseen you that existed from your first breath" (WL, 21).

40. Quoted in KS, p. 221

41. Ibid., p.222n and p. 147.

42. This phrase from Mallarmé's "Mimique" is employed by Derrida (DS, 175).

43. Antonin Artuad, *The Theater and Its Double*, trans. Mary Caroline Richards (New York: Grove Press, 1958), p. 9.

44. Quoted in Felicia H. Londré, *Tennessee Williams* (New York: Unger, 1979), p. 22.

45. *Tennessee Williams' Letters to Donald Windham, 1940–1965*, p. x.

46. *Lost Friendships*, pp. 265–66.

47. *This Sex*, p. 212.

48. Madison, *The Hermeneutics of Postmodernity*, p. 116.

49. Williams has explained that Blanche waiting for Mitch was the first image that came to him as he prepared to write the play: "Like I saw Blanche sitting in a chair with the moonlight coming through a window onto her. My first idea for a title was *Blanche's Chair in the Moon*. But I only wrote one scene then. She was waiting for Mitch, and he wasn't showing up" (CN, 215).

50. Roger Caillois, *Man, Play, and Games*, trans. M. Barash (New York: The Free Press), p. 12.

51. Definitions of "vertigo" and "simulation" here are taken from Peter Hutchinson, *Games Authors Play* (London and New York: Methuen), p. 6.

52. "Notebook for *A Streetcar Named Desire*," p. 369.

53. See St. Just, *Five O'Clock Angel*, p. 110.

54. Tennessee Williams himself has defended Blanche against charges that she was a liar: "I always thought she had her comic side, her little vanities, and her little white lies, but when it came to the nitty-gritty, she wasn't a liar. She told the truth when she had to. But she was broken on the rock of the world" (CN, 277).

55. Daniel Gerould, "Imaginary Invalids: A Theater of Simulated Patients" *Theater* 19, no. 1 (Fall–Winter, 1987): 13.

56. Ibid.

57. Bruce Wilshire, *Role Playing and Identity: The Limits of Theater as Metaphor* (Bloomington: Indiana University Press, 1982), p. 278.

58. On lying, Windham points out that "Tennessee once said in an interview that at a certain date he ceased to lie" (*Lost Friendships*, p. 216). Obviously such a claim can be trusted about as much as that of the Cretan liar.

59. Windham, *Lost Friendships*, p. 169.

60. Ibid., p. 194.

61. Ibid., p. 225; Windham's emphasis.

62. *Five O'clock Angel*, p. 282.

63. Bruce Smith, *Costly Performances Tennessee Williams: The Last Stage* (New York: Paragon House, 1990), p. 2.

64. Windham, *Lost Friendships*, p. 174.

65. Smith, *Costly Performances*, p. 2.

66. St. Just, *Five O'Clock Angel*, p. 262.

67. Ibid., p. 291

68. Ibid., p. 195.

69. David Wood, "Following Derrida," in *Deconstruction and Philosophy*, ed. John Sallis (Chicago: University of Chicago Press, 1987), p. 148.

Conclusion

1. *The Structuralist Controversy: The Languages of Criticism and the Sciences of Man*, eds. Richard Macksey and Eugenio Donato (Baltimore: Johns Hopkins University Press, 1972), p. 271.

Bibliography

Adler, Alfred. *A Streetcar Named Desire: The Moth and the Lantern*. Boston: Twayne, 1990.

Albee, Edward. *The Sandbox. The Death of Bessie Smith (with Fam and Yam)*. New York: Signet, 1963.

Altick, Richard D. *Lives and Letters: A History of Literature and Biography in England and America*. New York: Alfred A. Knopf, 1965.

Anderson, W. S. "The Orpheus of Virgil and Ovid: *flebile nescio quid*." In *Orpheus: The Metamorphoses of a Myth*, edited by John Warden, pp. 25–50. Toronto: The University of Toronto Press, 1982.

Artaud, Antonin. *The Theater and Its Double*. Translated by Mary and Caroline Richards. New York: Grove Press, 1958. Originally published as *Le Théâtre et son Double* (Paris: Gallimard, 1938).

Barthes, Roland. *Critical Essays*. Translated by Richard Howard. Evanston, Ill.: Northwestern University Press, 1972. Originally published as *Essais Critiques (Paris: Seuil, 1964)*

———. *Criticism and Truth*. Translated by Katrine Pilcher Keuneman. London: The Athlone Press, 1987. Originally published as *Critique et Vérité* (Paris: Seuil, 1966).

———. *Image-Music-Text*. Essays selected and translated by Stephen Heath. New York: Hill and Wang, 1977.

———. *The Pleasure of The Text*. Translated by Richard Miller. New York: Hill and Wang, 1975. Originally published as *Le Plaisir du Texte* (Paris: Seuil, 1973).

———. *Roland Barthes by Roland Barthes*. Translated by Richard Howard. New York: Hill and Wang, 1977. Originally published as *Roland Barthes par Roland Barthes* (Paris: Seuil, 1975).

———. *S/Z*. Translated by Richard Miller. New York: Hill and Wang, 1974. Originally published as *S/Z* (Paris: Seuil, 1970).

———. *Sade/Fourier/Loyola*. New York: Hill and Wang, 1976. Translated by Richard Miller. Originally published as *Sade, Fourier, Loyola* (Paris: Seuil, 1971).

———. "Theory of the Text." in *Untying the Text: A Post-Structuralist Reader*, edited by Robert Young, pp. 32–47. Boston: Routledge and Kegan Paul, 1981.

Bigsby, C. W. E. *A Critical Introduction to Twentieth Century Drama 2: Tennessee Williams, Arthur Miller, Edward Albee*. Cambridge: Cambridge University Press, 1984.

Bloom, Harold. *The Anxiety of Influence: A Theory of Poetry*. New York: Oxford University Press, 1973.

Bradbury, Malcolm. "The Telling Life: Some Thoughts on Literary Biography." In *The Troubled Face of Biography*, edited by Eric Homberger and John Charmley, pp. 131–40. Basingstoke: Macmillan, 1988.

Caillois, Roger. *Man, Play, and Games.* Translated by M. Barash. New York: Free Press of Glencoe, 1962.

Capote, Truman. "Remembering Tennessee." *Playboy* (January 1989); 228, 282.

Clifford, James. "'Hanging Up Looking Glasses at Odd Corners': Ethnobiographical Perspectives." In *Studies in Biography,* edited by Daniel Aaron, pp. 41–56. Cambridge: Harvard University Press, 1978.

Cohn, Ruby. "The Garrulous Grotesques of Tennessee Williams." In *Tennessee Williams: A Collection of Critical Essays,* edited by Stephen S. Stanton, pp. 45–60. Englewood Cliffs, N.J.: Prentice-Hall, 1977.

Dante, Alighieri. *The Divine Comedy of Dante Alighieri: Purgatorio.* Translated by Allen Mandelbaum. New York: Bantam, 1984.

Debusscher, Gilbert. "'Minting their Separate Wills': Tennessee Williams and Hart Crane." *Modern Drama* 26, no. 4 (1983): 455–76.

Denzin, Norman K. *Interpretive Biography.* Newbury Park, Calif.: Sage Publications, 1989.

Derrida, Jacques. "Coming into One's Own." In *Psychoanalysis and the Question of the Text: Selected Papers from the English Institute, 1976–1977,* edited by Geoffrey Hartman, pp. 114–148. Baltimore: The Johns Hopkins University Press, 1978.

———. *Dissemination.* Translated by Barbara Johnson. Chicago: University of Chicago Press, 1981. Originally published as *La dissémination* (Paris: Seuil, 1972).

———. *The Ear of the Other: Otobiography, Transference, Translation.* Translated by Peggy Kamuf. Lincoln: University of Nebraska Press, 1985. Originally published as *L'oreille de l'autre: otobiographies, transferts, traductions,* edited by Claude Lévesque and Christine V. Mcdonald (Montréal: VLB, 1982).

———. *Glas.* Translated by John P. Leavey, Jr., and Richard Rand. Lincoln: University of Nebraska Press, 1986. Originally published as *Glas* (Paris: Éditions Galilée, 1974).

———. *Margins of Philosophy.* Translated by Barbara Johnson. Chicago: University of Chicago Press, 1982. Originally published as *Marges: de la philosophie* (Paris: Minuit, 1972).

———. *Of Grammatology.* Translated by Gyatri Chakravorty Spivak. Baltimore: Johns Hopkins University Press, 1976. Originally published as *De la Grammatologie* (Paris: Minuit, 1967).

———. *Positions.* Translated by Alan Bass. Chicago: University of Chicago Press, 1981.

———. *Signéponge/Signsponge.* Translated by Richard Rand. New York: Columbia University Press, 1984.

———. *Writing and Difference.* Translated by Alan Bass. Chicago: University of Chicago Press, 1981. Originally published as *L'écriture et la différence* (Paris: Seuil, 1967).

Dervin, Daniel A. "The Spook in the Rainforest: The Incestuous Structure of Tennessee Williams's Plays." *Psychocultural Review* 3 (Summer–Fall 1979): 158–83.

Devlin, Albert J., ed. *Conversations with Tennessee Williams.* Jackson: University Press of Mississippi, 1986.

Ditsky, John. *The Onstage Christ: Studies in the Persistance of a Theme.* Totawa, N.J.: Barnes and Noble, 1980.

Donahue, Francis. *The Dramatic World of Tennessee Williams.* New York: Ungar, 1964.

Dronke, Peter. "The Return of Eurydice." *Classica et Mediaevalia* 23 (1962): 198–215.

Edel, Leon. "Biography and the Science of Man." In *New Directions in Biography.* Edited by Antony M. Friedson, pp. 1–11. Manoa: University of Hawaii Press, 1981.

———. "The Figure Under the Carpet." In *Telling Lives: The Biographer's Art,* edited by Marc Pachter, pp. 16–34. Washington, D.C.: New Republic, 1979.

———. *Literary Biography.* Toronto: Toronto University Press, 1957. Reprint. Bloomington: Indiana University Press, 1973.

———. *Writing Lives: principia biographica.* New York: Norton, 1984.

Falk, Signi L. *Tennessee Williams.* 2d ed. Boston: Twayne/G.K. Hall, 1978.

Foucault, Michel. *The History of Sexuality, Volume 1: An Introduction.* Translated by Robert Hurley. New York: Vintage Books, 1980. Originally published as *La Volonté de savoir* (Paris: Gallimard, 1976).

———. *The History of Sexuality, Volume 2: The Use of Pleasure.* Translated by Robert Hurley. New York: Vintage Books, 1985. Originally published as *L'Usage des Plaisirs* (Paris: Gallimard, 1984).

Ganz, Arthur. "The Desperate Morality of the Plays of Tennessee Williams." In *Tennessee Williams: A Collection of Critical Essays,* edited by Stephen S. Stanton, pp. 123–37. Englewood Cliffs, N.J.: Prentice-Hall, 1977.

Gass, William. "Mr. Blotner, Mr. Feaster, and Mr. Faulkner." *New York Review of Books,* 27 June 1974: 3–5.

Genet, Jean. *The Balcony.* Translated by Bernard Frechtman. New York: Grove Press, 1958.

Gerould, Daniel. "Imaginary Invalids: A Theater of Simulated Patients." *Theater* 19, no. 1 (Fall–Winter 1987): 6–18.

Gould, Jean. *Modern American Playwrights.* New York: Dodd, Mead, 1966.

Graves, Robert. *The Greek Myths: 1.* London: Penguin, 1955.

Guthrie, W. K. C. *Orpheus and the Greek Religion: A Study of the Orphic Movement.* Rev. ed. New York: Norton, 1966.

Handy, W. C., ed. *The Treasury of the Blues: Complete Words and Music of 67 Great Songs from Memphis to the Present Day with an Historical and Critical Text by Abbe Niles.* 2d ed. New York: Charles Boni, 1949.

Hirsch, Foster. *A Portrait of the Artist: the Plays of Tennessee Williams.* Port Washington, N.Y.: Kennikat Press, 1979.

Holroyd, Michael. "How I Fell Into Biography." In Eric Homberger and John Charmley, *The Troubled Face of Biography,* pp. 94–103. Basingstoke: Macmillan, 1988.

Homberger, Eric, and John Charmley, eds., *The Troubled Face of Biography.* Basingstoke: Macmillan, 1988.

Hurley, Paul J. "Tennessee Williams: the Playwright as Social Critic." *The Theater Annual* 21 (1964): 40–56.

Hutchinson, Peter. *Games Authors Play.* London and New York: Methuen, 1983.

Hyman, Stanley Edgar. "Some Notes on the Albertine Strategy." *Hudson Review* 6 (Autumn 1953): 417–22.

Irigaray, Luce. *This Sex Which Is Not One.* Translated by Catherine Porter with Carolyn Burke. Ithaca: Cornell University Press, 1985. Originally published as *Ce Sexe qui n'est pas un* (Paris: Editions de Minuit, 1977).

Jackson, Ester M. *The Broken World of Tennessee Williams*. Madison: University of Wisconsin Press, 1966.

Jay, Paul L. "Being in the Text: Autobiography and the Problem of the Subject." *MLN* 97, no. 4 (December 1982): 1045–1063.

———. "What's the Use? Critical Theory and the Study of Autobiography." *Biography* 10, no. 1 (Winter 1987): 39–54.

Jones, LeRoi. *Blues People: Negro Music in White America*. New York: William Morrow, 1963.

Kamuf, Peggy. *Signature Pieces: On the Institution of Authorship*. Ithaca: Cornell University Press, 1988.

Kaplan, Justin. "The 'Real Life.'" In *Studies in Biography*. Edited by Daniel Aaron, pp. 1–8. Cambridge: Harvard University Press, 1978.

Kazan, Elia. "Notebook for *A Streetcar Named Desire*." In *Directors on Directing: A Source Book for Modern Theater*. Edited by Toby Cole and Helen Krick Chinoy. Indianapolis and New York: Bobbs-Merril, 1976.

Kendall, Paul Murray. *The Art of Biography*. New York: Norton, 1965.

Kristeva, Julia. *Desire in Language: A Semiotic Approach to Literature and Art*, edited by Leon S. Roudiez. Translated by Thomas Gora, Alice Jardine, and Leon S. Roudiez. New York: Columbia University Press, 1980.

———. *Sémeiotiké: Recherches pour une sémanalyse*. Paris: Editions du Seuil, 1969.

Leavey, John P., Jr. *Glassary*. Lincoln: University of Nebraska Press, 1986.

Londré, Felicia H. *Tennessee Williams*. New York: Unger, 1979.

Macksey, Richard, and Eugenio Donato, eds. *The Structuralist Controversy: The Languages of Criticism and the Sciences of Man*. Baltimore: Johns Hopkins University Press, 1972.

Madison, G. B. *The Hermeneutics of Postmodernity: Figures and Themes*. Bloomington and Indianapolis: Indiana University Press, 1988.

Malamud, Bernard. *Dubin's Lives*. New York: Farrar, Straus and Giroux, 1979.

Mordden, Ethan. *The American Theater*. New York: Oxford University Press, 1981.

Nadel, Ira Bruce. *Biography: Fiction, Fact, and Form*. New York: St. Martin's, 1984.

Nelson, Benjamin. *Tennessee Williams: His Life and Work*. New York: Obolensky, 1961.

Norris, Christopher. *Deconstruction and the Interests of Theory*. London: Printers Publishers, 1988.

Novarr, David. *The Lines of Life: Theories of Biography, 1880–1970*. West Lafayette, Ind.: Purdue University Press, 1986.

Oliver, Paul. *Conversation with the Blues*. New York: Horizon Press, 1986.

Ovid. *Metamorphoses*. Edited by E. J. Kenney. Translated by A. D. Melville. Oxford and New York: Oxford University Press, 1986.

Parker, R. B. "The Circle Closed: A Psychological Reading of *The Glass Menagerie* and *The Two-Character Play*." *Modern Drama* 28, no. 4 (December 1985): 517–34.

Petrie, Dennis W. *Ultimately Fiction: Design in Modern American Literary Biography*. West Lafayette, Ind.: Purdue University Press, 1981.

Phillips, Gene D. *The Films of Tennessee Williams*. Philadelphia: Art Alliance Press; London and Toronto: Associated University Presses, 1980.

Plottel, Jeanine Parisier, and Hanna Charney. *Intertextuality: New Perspectives in Criticism*. New York: New York Literary Forum, 1978.

Poe, Edgar Allan. *The Poems of Edgar Allan Poe.* Edited by Killis Campbell. New York: Russel and Russel, 1962.

Preston, Jerry, ed. *Blues Lyric Poetry.* New York: Garland Publishing, 1983.

Quirino, Leonard. "The Cards Indicate a Voyage on *A Streetcar Named Desire.*" In *Tennessee Williams: A Tribute.* Edited by Jac Tharpe, pp. 77–96. Jackson: University Press of Mississippi, 1977.

Rader, Dotson. *Tennessee: Cry of the Heart.* New York: Doubleday, 1985.

Rilke, Rainer Maria. *Duino Elegies and The Sonnets to Orpheus.* Translated by A. Poulin, Jr. Boston: Houghton Mifflin, 1977.

Robbins, Emmet. "Famous Orpheus." In *Orpheus: The Metamorphoses of a Myth.* Edited by John Warden. Toronto and Buffalo: University of Toronto Press, 1982.

Rogers, Ingrid. *Tennessee Williams: A Moralist's Answer to the Problems of Life.* Frankfurt: Peter Lang Frankfurt/M. Herbert Lang Bern, 1976.

Rose, Phyllis. *Woman of Letters: A Life of Virginia Woolf.* New York: Oxford University Press, 1978.

St. Just, Maria. *Five O'Clock Angel: Letters of Tennessee Williams to Maria St. Just 1948–1982.* New York: Alfred A. Knopf, 1990.

Sarotte, George-Michel. *Like a Brother, Like a Lover: Male Homosexuality in the American Novel and Theatre from Herman Melville to James Baldwin.* Translated by Richard Miller. Garden City, N.Y.: Anchor Press/Doubleday, 1978.

Searle, John. *Speech Acts: An Essay in the Philosophy of Language.* London: Cambridge University Press, 1969.

Sievers, W. David. *Freud on Broadway.* New York: Hermitage House, 1955.

Slinn, E. Warwick. "Deconstruction and Meaning: The Textuality Game." *Philosophy and Literature* 12, no. 1 (April 1988): 80–87.

Smith, Bruce. *Costly Performances Tennessee Williams: The Last Stage.* New York: Paragon House, 1990.

Sontag, Susan. "Writing Itself: On Roland Barthes." In *Barthes: Selected Writings,* edited by Susan Sontag. New York: Hill and Wang, 1982.

Spoto, Donald. *The Kindness of Strangers: The Life of Tennessee Williams.* Boston: Little, Brown and Co., 1985.

Stanton, Stephen S., ed. *Tennessee Williams: A Collection of Critical Essays.* Englewood Cliffs, N.J.: Prentice-Hall, 1977.

Steen, Mike. *A Look at Tennessee Williams.* New York: Hawthorne Books, 1969.

Tharpe, Jac, ed. *Tennessee Williams: A Tribute.* Jackson: University Press of Mississippi, 1977.

Tischler, Nancy M. *Tennessee Williams: Rebellious Puritan.* New York: Citadel Press, 1961.

Todd, Jean Marie. *Autobiographics in Freud and Derrida.* New York: Garland Publishing, 1990.

Ulmer, Gregory L. *Teletheory: Grammatology in the Age of Video.* New York: Routledge, 1989.

Virgil. *The Georgics and Eclogues of Virgil.* Translated by T. C. Williams. Cambridge: Harvard University Press, 1915.

Vlasopolos, Anca. "Authorizing History: Victimization in *A Streetcar Named Desire.*" *Theatre Journal* (October 1986): 322–38.

Warden, John, ed. *Orpheus: The Metamorphoses of a Myth*. Toronto and Buffalo: University of Toronto Press, 1982.

Weales, Gerald. *Tennessee Williams*. Minneapolis: University of Minnesota Press, 1965.

Williams, Dakin, and Shepherd Mead. *Tennessee Williams: An Intimate Biography*. New York: Arbor House, 1983.

Williams, Edwina Dakin, and Lucy Freeman. *Remember Me to Tom*. New York: Putnam, 1963.

Williams, Tennessee. *American Blues: Five Short Plays*. New York: Dramatists Play Service, 1948. (Includes *Moony's Kid Don't Cry, The Long Stay Cut Short, or, The Unsatisfactory Supper, The Case of the Crushed Petunias, Ten Blocks on the Camino Real, The Dark Room*.)

————. *Camino Real*. New York: New Directions, 1970.

————. *Cat on a Hot Tin Roof*. New York: Signet, 1985.

————. *Collected Stories*. New York: New Directions, 1985.

————. *Four Plays: Summer and Smoke, Orpheus Descending, Suddenly Last Summer, and Period of Adjustment*. New York: Signet, 1976.

————. *In the Winter of Cities*. New York: New Directions, 1964.

————. Introduction. *The Dark at the Top of the Stairs*. By William Inge. New York: Random House, 1958. vii–ix.

————. *The Glass Menagerie*. New York: New Directions, 1970.

————. "Man Named Tennessee." *Newsweek* 1 (April 11, 1957): 81.

————. *Memoirs*. New York: Doubleday, 1975.

————. *Moise and the World of Reason*. New York: Bantam, 1976.

————. *Orpheus Descending with Battle of Angels*. New York: New Directions, 1958.

————. *A Streetcar Named Desire*. New York: Signet, 1984.

————. *Three by Tennessee: Sweet Bird of Youth, The Rose Tattoo, and The Night of the Iguana*. New York: Signet, 1976.

————. *27 Wagons Full of Cotton and Other One Act Plays*, New York: New Directions, 1976. (Includes *The Purification* and *The Long Goodbye*)

————. *The Two-Character Play*, New York: New Directions, 1979.

————. *Where I Live: Selected Essays*, New York: New Directions, 1978.

Windham, Donald, ed. *Tennessee Williams' Letters to Donald Windham, 1940–1965*. New York: Holt, Rinehart, and Winston, 1976.

————. *Lost Friendships: A Memoir of Truman Capote, Tennessee Williams, and Others*. New York: William Morrow, 1983.

Wilshire, Bruce. *Role Playing and Identity: The Limits of Theatre as Metaphor*. Bloomington: Indiana University Press, 1982.

Wood, David. "Following Derrida." In *Deconstruction and Philosophy*. Edited by John Sallis. Chicago: University of Chicago Press, 1987.

Zuber, Ortrun. "The Translation of Non-Verbal Signs in Drama." *Pacific Quarterly* 5 (1980): 61–74.

Index